Soul to Soul takes the reader into the spiritual world of a guru, revealing layer after layer of the evolution to enlightenment. This book also provides such thought-provoking material that one is compelled to look beyond the soul's façade to ultimately learn how to become one with the universal soul created by God in the beginning. The great divide and the chaos that proliferates in the world today is evidence of the disconnection of mankind "soul to soul." We need a way back from the path of destruction. Experience the Challenge of *Soul to Soul*.

—Raheema Turner Shabazz, author, *Trials and Triumphs of the Downtrodden*, *Born Again*, and *White Collar Nightmare*

"When the student is ready the Master appears." Such is the case with Kitabu Turner Roshi, a Master/Teacher. You walk away knowing you've had a remarkable sharing. His personal encounters from prejudice and police brutality to guru will lead you through the illusion, showing a way closer to the realization of Nothing/No-Mind and Enlightenment.

—Geo (The Hands) Emory, artist

Also by Vernon Kitabu Turner

Kung Fu: The Master
The Secret of Freedom
Soul Sword: The Way and Mind of a Zen Warrior

SOUL TO SOUL

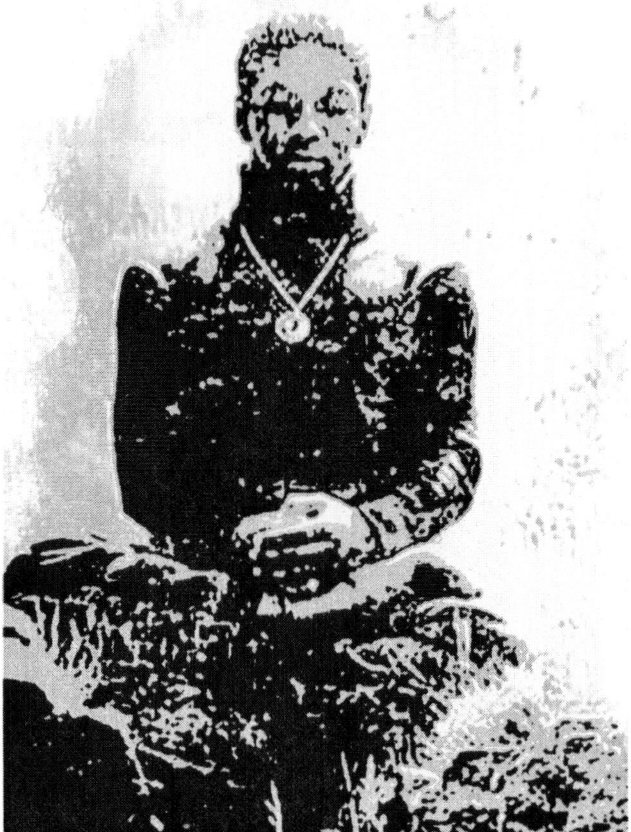

Harnessing the Power of Your Mind

VERNON KITABU TURNER, ROSHI

Cover design and digital enhancement by Anne Dunn Louque
Cover photo by Henry Foster

Hampton Roads Publishing Company, Inc.
1125 Stoney Ridge Road
Charlottesville, VA 22902

434-296-2772
fax: 434-296-5096
e-mail: hrpc@hrpub.com
www.hrpub.com

If you are unable to order this book from your local
bookseller, you may order directly from the publisher.
Call 1-800-766-8009, toll-free.

Library of Congress Cataloging-in-Publication Data

Turner, Vernon Kitabu, 1948-
Soul to soul : harnessing the power of your mind / Vernon Kitabu Turner.
p. cm.
ISBN 1-57174-470-3 (pbk. : alk. paper)
1. Religious life--Zen Buddhism. 2. Meditation--Zen Buddhism. I. Title.
BQ9286.T87 2006
294.3'444--dc22

2006005147

ISBN 1-57174-470-3
10 9 8 7 6 5 4 3 2 1
Printed on acid-free paper in Canada

Dedication

How can you learn without a teacher?

To my parents, Vernon and Kate Ely Turner, who by teaching me the Way of Christ upheld the faith that God can and does indwell man. Dedicated to Robert C13X, Zen master Nomura Roshi, and Sadguru Sant Keshavadas who pointed directly to Universal Mind in me. To my sister in the Way, Deborah Thomas of Third Baptist Church, Portsmouth, Virginia, who never once doubted my calling from childhood to today, and to Pastor Anne T. Barnes of Grace Temple/Fruit of the Spirit Church, Norfolk, Virginia, who opened the door for the roshi to teach the transformation of the Mind in the House of God. A special dedication to my uncles James and Bishop Joseph Ely for their love and to my aunt Mildred Ely for speaking to me only in the Spirit, so that that I always knew that she knew that I knew that she knew what was really going on when we stood face to face. Thanks, Aunt Mildred. To God be the glory for the thing He has done. I am but a vessel, a bold witness to what is so. I am a living soul, the very breath of God. This form is but particles of dust . . . whoosh! I am not that. You are not that. We are something exceedingly greater.

Last, but in no way least, I thank my wife Joyce Anne, in whose presence the mind of both the writer and the roshi can flourish.

Contents

1

The Thinking Mind

You have only to close your eyes and all that you see vanishes into a void. In deep silence and darkness, you have only your thoughts to assure you that there is a world and living people in it. Man has come to rely on thoughts as the most precious tool. Yet, whereas the medium of thought is wondrous when consciously applied by the thinker, it can be the cause of misery and destruction when manipulated by a mind not his own.

Human beings are far more than flesh and blood. There is more to us than can be measured by machines or viewed under a microscope. Scientific minds are studying something, but is the body really what we are? The planet has been repopulated countless times. In a hundred or more years, every one of the six billion people here now will only be a memory in the brain of a relative who is on his or her way to the same fate.

So what is being alive really about? Is it that we come from and go into oblivion? If that is so, then life is utterly meaningless. It would render all the lofty thoughts and achievements of our kind virtually pointless; celebrated histories and storied greatness would be delusions shared by the remaining masses, also waiting to be erased from existence. What does it really matter that others will remember you, if there is nothing of you that remains in your consciousness to know you ever passed this way?

There are many religions that purport to answer our questions. They give us hope and dreams of a better life beyond this. They reach out to the source of our being, a source we think we can capture in a name or title. He is God, Lord, Jehovah, Allah, and He is not. In Asia and Africa, the feminine aspect of the Godhead is also embraced. How we approach this mystery of our own being determines whether or not we will attain the answer that will set us free.

In searching to connect to that part of us we sense is missing, some of us focus on worship, some on reading the Scriptures; others on keeping the tenets of a chosen faith; that is, we try hard to be good. There are still others of us who take a more doctrinaire approach, acquiring information about the Lord. Whatever we know, however we approach the subject does not seem to make us loving human beings. Christians are fond of quoting the Scripture, "Peace on earth," "Good will toward men," during the Christmas season. Israelis use the word "Shalom," whereas Arabs use "Salaam." Everyone is evoking the mantra of peace, yet where is the peace? Obviously, the peace that is indicated does not arise from our thoughts, nor from our belief that it is possible.

There is, indeed, far more to you than can be seen, but you cannot unlock that secret by studying the physical body. You cannot come into the fullness of that experience merely by linking yourself to an organized group. There are some roads you must travel alone.

You are a prodigal child. You are a long way from your true home and no boat, train, or plane can take you there. You are being called. Perhaps you have felt the vibration, like the persistent buzz of your cell phone, but you couldn't tell where it was coming from.

You are loved. You are not loved for what you have made of yourself or for anything you've done. You are loved just because you're you. It is like the love your mother felt when she held you in her arms for the first time, only immeasurably greater.

Love is calling you, but it is not calling your body. It is calling you, the very essence of itself. Love is calling to pure love.

You may not feel like pure love or perfection because you have a mind to remember your misdeeds. This is no accident. You meditate on your shortcomings and lack of perfection because you have been manipulated into thinking that you are supposed to.

You may know the law of man, you may think you understand the commandments, but do you get the point, the hidden meaning behind the Scriptures?

It is to be expected that when people speak of the soul, they think of religion and the salvation of this "thing" they know nothing about. Souls go to heaven or hell—that's it, end of discussion . . . or so we are led to think.

Suppose that is only a shadow of the truth. Suppose souls go to the mall, baseball games, concerts, and swimming while sharing all of it with God Himself. Suppose a soul could do that.

The ways of God are not the ways of humankind. As creatures of free will, we have thought ourselves into a jam that we cannot think ourselves out of. We have needed help for a long time, and help has always been available. We are like a person holding a bottle of nitroglycerin while preparing to jump a hurdle. We do not understand the power of thought, nor do we comprehend the relationship of thought to the mind that fires those thoughts from "nowhere" into consciousness.

Misdirected thought is dangerous to the life of a soul. If such a man is to be saved, another man must be willing to risk his life.

The human being is marvelously formed. The part that is visible is also the part that can be readily studied. We are also, however, mysterious beings. Every culture through every century had a type of priesthood. A "priest" is an intermediary between the Spirit and humankind. Spirit is beyond thought.

Religion can be studied. Spirituality is not the words about it. Spirituality is what results from transformation. No biblical hero was more proof of this teaching than Apostle Paul, who said, "Be not conformed to the image of the world but be ye transformed by the renewing of your mind."

These words were uttered after his own mindset was overturned by direct contact with the voice of Christ. Speaking directly to individual listeners, he said not to concentrate on or pattern yourself after the things you see. Work on renewing your mind. You will be transformed.

Zen Buddhism purports to be a direct pointing at the soul, not dependent on words and letters. There are also many Zen teachings that warn the disciple not to focus on images, even if that image appears to be the Lord himself. Ironically, despite popular usage, Zen is not a school of Buddhism. It is beyond such designations and is accessible to everyone with a soul.

Your body is an image in the world. So what would happen if you did not attach to it as you have always done? What if you stopped seeing other people as body types? What would happen?

Now, this practice—the practice that comes with the endorsement of Jesus himself and numerous Zen masters and gurus—of letting go of form throws us a curve. If you are a Christian, the message is to let go of the image, if you want transformation. What image?

News flash! The image you have of Jesus, whether from a painting or your imagination, is not Jesus. It is a mere icon. Is your faith strong enough to drop the image to connect with the truth behind it?

I have a rare Buddha that was given to me as a gift by Lin Zhang-Yuan Ling, a Chinese-language professor of my nephew Pedro S. Silva, a poet. Lin is also a master of kung fu, as is her husband, John. She belongs to the largest Buddhist group in the world, Compassion Relief Tzu Chi Foundation, headed by the Venerable Dharma Master, Chen Yen. I stood before the Buddha shrine in her home and gave a bow of respect. I did not bow to an artistic rendering of a historic figure. I bowed spontaneously to the living truth for which the statue stood. It was an experience I was having inwardly, but the others in the room felt something also.

"The Buddha wants to go home with you," Lin said, and promptly began looking for a box. It was significant moment.

"It is time for me to go beyond images," she said.

Whereas I have no attachment to the Buddha image, I was aware of the significance of my Chinese counterparts sharing the antique statue. I received the gift as a message from our original ancestors. It now sits on the altar in the American Vishwa Dharma Zendo with a cross and other gifts or symbols of faith.

The Buddha wanted to go home with a man of African roots. The Buddha is neither a statue nor the man.

The Buddha is the Universal Mind itself. It passes from culture to culture, soul to soul, fulfilling its mission. As I watched the Buddha statue

being prepared for me, I recognized how marvelously orchestrated were the lives of those chosen to fulfill the will of God. The vision of my mission as expressed by my guru was unfolding. "Not me, not me"—I understood that it was not that I myself was worthy of any special honor, but that I was somehow an ambassador of the Way, regardless. The ambassador represents the power. He himself is not the power. It pleased me when others paid respect to the "hidden" master. I knew it meant that the time was nearing when the Light would shine brightly through the dark corridors of the mind.

In places of worship, we pay lip service to the unseen, Yet in our daily lives, we lose touch with our source. Do not conform to images. There is something more. We don't have the same talents; we don't do the same jobs. It has been said that God specializes. If that much is accepted, it should be no surprise that God would have specialists. It is the job of these specialists to uphold the unseen in the everyday world.

In America and other Western societies, the church and its ministers have been part of the community for centuries. Preachers are seen as workers for God and they do their jobs in the open. Unfortunately, though God is praised as spirit, strengthening the spirit of the believer, rare indeed is it for any believer of the West to give any serious consideration to the Mind aspect of God. Consequently, not only the virtue of this spiritual practice but also the mission of those whom God ordains to teach it is basically unknown or feared as the product of a foreign religion. It is common for the preacher to condemn what he does not understand. This produces a divided house. One hand upholds the Lord as the sacrificial lamb while the other hand denies the Lord as master teacher. A master is different from a preacher. A preacher inspires a person to make a decision. The master teaches a person how to transform into the likeness of himself, to be a master also. It is possible for people to master the course, but not if they do not understand that it is their duty to reach higher. Salvation is a gift. There is no reward attached to the mere act of seeking redemption. Redemption is what is given. Illumination, enlightenment, awakening the mind, take the kind of faith that encounters and overcomes many obstacles along the way. Those who would attain the Mind are spiritual warriors.

Enlightenment is something that can only be achieved by a living being. Even though your soul/spirit is set free at the death of your body, the release occurs involuntarily. When the soul is realized while you are still alive to the body, something incredible occurs. You are living spirit while still walking the earth. Soul constitutes your personal identity. Spirit is the life current itself. Your mind is the medium that binds or frees you. It is one thing to be "born of the spirit," but when your mind and spirit meet through the medium of the soul in the body, you become a living soul, the very definition of the first man.

After enlightenment, your body is still serviceable, but you wear it like an outer coat. This is the beginning. The world is brand new for you.

God chooses those He wants to teach, and that is the end of it. No one can say why. If that person happens to be you, your life will be anything but easy. The solitary spiritual votary, meditating quietly, living in the stillness within, is common in the East. There is a rich history that goes back thousands of years. What if God instilled such a Mind in a person born in the West? What if no one suspected or even expected such an arrival?

I am a loner,
I stand and walk alone,
Though I travel the endless road,
I call no place my home,
For the life of one such as I
Is never spent one place,
And I am fated to wander
Until death has stilled my pace
Though I travel this road.
Neither do I know,
From whence the power comes,
Or whither I must go.

—Vernon Kitabu Turner (written at age 14),
Kung Fu: The Master

When you are Chosen, the spirit bears silent witness over and over again while you learn. If you do not believe, you will be made to believe. There is nowhere to escape. As the Spirit of God incarnated in Christ, He continues to flow from soul to soul through the power of the Holy Spirit. Now is the time of the Mind. The soul cannot break free from the delusion that binds it to the great lie while our minds remain under the sway of the world of form. It cannot break free until it harmonizes with Universal Mind. Meditate on this! Should you really be surprised that the God who sent forth His spirit housed in men to reach men would also send forth His Mind in men to reach men?

"I have sheep that ye know not of," Jesus said. Jesus also said something else that is curious, considering how divided are the world's people: "If I be lifted up I will draw *all men* unto me" [italics mine]. So Jesus was working for all men, according to his view. That would rule out exclusivity.

When one receives the Spirit of God while maintaining carnal mind, the results from the experience are distorted by the mind itself. Mind is the enemy of the Spirit. The Original Mind is one with the spirit. In its current state, your mind blocks the full expression of your being. It keeps you operating in a world of limitations.

Most people are born. Those who are emissaries of the Universal Mind are "unborn." This is the mind of the guru and the Zen master. The guru is linked to the Lord from the womb. He learns about the world as he goes. The Zen master is one who achieves the connection along the road of life, and applies Original Mind to day-to-day activity.

Gurus usually focus on the spirit/supernatural link whereas Zen masters apply spirituality to ordinary life. It is a matter of focus. Jesus Christ said, "I am come that ye might have life and have it more abundantly." Abundant life sounds good. This was not a promise to Christians because Jesus had already stated he was working for humanity as a whole. It was a promise to humanity. So where is the abundant life?

"How will they learn without a teacher?" (Apostle Paul, Romans 10:14)

You have to apply the teachings to get the results.

If you have some insight into the inner workings of the emissaries of Universal Mind, it will help you search out your own true being. You do not have a soul. You are the soul. If you are not living from the true center of being, it is because you have not been taught to recognize your true self in the midst of all the "Hollywood lights."

The truth will set you free. Come walk with me. Stop concentrating on your body. Come as a child would come, walking hand in hand with a trusted friend or parent. Forget your mind. We are taking a journey on the spiritual network, soul to soul. Your mind cannot enter.

If you are a person of faith, it is a good time to pray for guidance. The truth will bear witness to itself. If you approach this subject from a Judeo-Christian or other God-centered approach, you may expect certain things. If you fancy yourself a Zen person, you may also expect a certain language and familiarity to be found within these pages. This book will only help you if you read it as truth. It may defy logic, it may raise questions about the way you ordinarily think, but that is its purpose, to drive you beyond the realm of thought. If there is no witness, if the Spirit of Truth does not speak to your spirit, use this book for doggy paper, with my blessings.

II

To Some He Sent Teachers: The Christian and the Guru

Sadguru Sant Keshavadas, "the singing saint of India," transmitted Dharma (the Law of the Spirit) to me in 1977. He publicly revealed that God had chosen me to be a guru, a spiritual teacher. I was already well known in some quarters as poet and Zen martial artist. My poetry book, *Kung Fu: The Master* (Donning, 1975), had the unintended effect of establishing me as an enigma in the martial arts world and among some Zen pundits and Christians, as well. By the time I met Guruji, I had already experienced profound satori twice. Satori is a direct spiritual breakthrough, an enlightenment experience. While on the surface, it appeared that I had become Buddhist, the fact was there was no internal division between my lifetime of Christian experience and the path being revealed to me.

There was, however, a major difference in the way this spiritual teacher approached me, as compared to all the preachers I had known. Guruji, like my roshi before him, communed with me without words. Words were optional. His manner of teaching me was telepathic. That got my attention. It connected with something hidden deep inside me. It was not like Guruji was telling me anything. He was like a spiritual mirror allowing me to see what I could not see at first. He was reflecting something back that was familiar to me in a mystical way.

Even though I had experienced satori, I humbled myself and sat at the feet of the Himalayan master. I recognized the spirit in him. He felt like someone I talked to almost every day of my life. In him, I felt the spirit of my father—not the father of my body, the father of my soul. Sensing this so completely (words fail to explain the depth of the feeling), I melted inside, I yielded. You may think you are above the teacher and further teachings but you delude yourself. No one is ever above the teacher because the spirit of the teacher is God Himself. When the teacher needs the Teacher, someone appears even for him. There is a time to stand strong. There is a time to bow. I learned it is wise to bow and pay respect to whomever God sends to help.

Learning that I had a guru disturbed my mother greatly. She was a woman so grounded in Christ and the gospel that, as children, my siblings and I joked that on the last day we would grab her feet and hitch a ride to heaven just in case we didn't qualify for the trip on our own. I respected my mother's relationship with God. Kate Ely Turner was the daughter of a West Indian bishop named Joseph Ely. Her love of the Lord was openly displayed in public and private the whole of my life. When it came to searching the Scriptures, I relied on her understanding until she entered the courtyard of grace in April 2000.

Despite my recognition of her spiritual standing, when it came to what was happening to me in my inner practice, the Zen bent of my approach to God and my relationship to Guruji, I knew that I was on a path that was not within her realm of understanding. "It is not given to all to know the mystery," the Scriptures read. I knew I, alone, was responsible to be true to the path the One Lord revealed to me. It was not obvious at the time, due to various circumstances, but through the power of reflection I can now see that my life was being orchestrated. I was following a rhythm that did not come from the outer world. For a long time, there had been no one to talk to but the Invisible Lord Himself. Now there was Sadguru Sant Keshavadas. To sit with him was enough. I had no questions to ask. They were all answered in our silent communion.

My mother fondly called me her "peculiar" child. She talked to Jesus.

Though I also recognized Jesus, my communication was always directed to the One behind him, the Father, as in "Our Father" of the prayer. From infancy, I had heard the prayer and been taught about the reality of God. That I accepted it as a matter of course seems as natural as accepting my human parents. Never in all of my life have I had a single moment of doubt about the existence of God. My questions were reserved for what we are fond of calling "the real world." I was certain that I knew when God was leading me. I wanted Him to lead me. That is the first key to spiritual advancement. You must tone down your ego. You must deflate your intellect. There is a gate, but knowledge cannot take you through it. There comes a time when the most brilliant mind must bow to the Greater. The Teacher is greater.

The teacher is the master who stays on the lower plain of existence out of compassion. His mission is to *show* the way. Those who are chosen to follow in his wake must be in his likeness. They are to function in the same spirit and mind. They are not imitators. They are very real, but very different, like offspring of the same parents can be. The commonality is that they have the same root as the master. They, too, are motivated by cosmic love.

When the pupil is ready, the teacher will appear.

Though I had received my "shingle" to teach in 1977, I did not want to. Though I could not run from that duty completely, I did not make it easy for people to find me. I remained devoted to my beloved friend and mentor, martial arts master C. O. Neal, until his death and was a humble disciple of the Sadguru until he left the earth also. I found joy in serving the masters. It seemed vital that I support them in their work. I did not want to take the high seat myself. I was more or less forced out into the open. I had nowhere to hide when Santji (my more familiar term for Guruji) left us. Yet Santji did not leave me without support.

In 1977, he wrote under the seal of the Vishwa Shanti Temple: "By the authority of God within me, I authorize Kitabu Kaivalya Shyam (Vernon Kitabu Turner) to teach, Dhyana (Zen), Bhakti Yoga (Devotion to God) and Jnana Yoga (The Yoga of wisdom). May he serve humanity with Om and Prem."

With that, he ordained me as an emissary of the Vishwa Dharma under the blessings of the Vishwa Shanti Temple in the Himalayas. It was not an honor, not in the world I lived in. The designation was a mountain to climb. Yet the beloved master did not speak or write idly. He was an instrument, not the source, so I had to learn to receive the message in faith.

Santji had no fear in acting on the revelation. There were times when devotees gathered to hear the master speak and he called me to teach instead. This puzzled the assembly, and some of them were bold enough to ask why. The last time Santji was in Virginia, he spoke at the Hindu Temple in Chesapeake. When I entered, he was seated on the "lotus throne." He pointed to me and said, "Kitabu is one of the great disciples of the Himalayan masters." Then he motioned for me to come and sit next to him. When he was served food, he held the plate and fed me. What is curious about this from the logical view is that I never went to the Himalayas physically. Many of his devotees, some of them known to me, went with Santji to India. I never made the trip in my body. The spiritual teacher is not communicating with your body.

When these honors were bestowed on me, I received them as a representative, an ambassador. As Guruji was a realized soul of India, I knew that I was being groomed to be a realized soul free to express that unique spiritual genius of my own people. I was born in the West. There was no understanding or precedence for such a mission of guru or roshi here in America. What was I to do? What was I to think about all of this?

Guruji helped. "Not-I, Not-I," he always said when he was credited with some accomplishment. When honor was being bestowed, I understood that I was not the recipient, I was simply the icon in that moment, standing for the One who remained unseen.

There is something big at work behind the person of the guru. Guruji wanted to make sure that I "got it." He did not play to politics. Millionaires and famous people courted him. I was just a young poet of minor means, but I always had his ear—always. Lightning was flashing from the East to the West. In the eyes of Guruji, I saw the brilliancy. He made sure I understood—the lightning was flashing back.

God moves in mysterious ways. As a young boy, I was compelled to pray that he make me an instrument of His peace and love. Whatever was happening was not being controlled by me. I was learning about the nature of the guru from inside the experience. It seems important that those born in countries where such a spiritual office is largely unknown learn what it is. No scholar can help you understand. One who is living the experience can garner poetic images of that which is largely unspeakable. It will give you a sense of the truth of it. To connect with this truth may help you respect the representative. You would not want to see what lies behind the eyes of the guru.

Like all disciples who are ordained to carry forth the teachings, the offspring takes off in a slightly different direction, suitable to his or her own nature and background. Sadguru Sant Keshavadas taught the Vishwa Dharma to the Western world through the Temples of Cosmic Religion he founded worldwide. People from every religion and philosophy freely came to study. I teach under the banner of the American Vishwa Dharma Zen Mission. It was clear to me that the teachings of the Dharma are part of the healing balm God prepared for nations. The Dharma needed those who understood it enough to speak to a different people. I recognized how much fellow Christians, Americans in general, and African Americans specifically, could benefit from the inner teachings.

I gave myself fully to the mission, noting occasionally that my life was beginning to take on features similar to that of Santji (Guruji) himself. I wrestled with the trappings that came with the responsibility. Christians, as a rule, are not taught that there can be mastery or a master outside of Jesus Christ. This one misconception constitutes a major mountain of deceit.

Extraordinary things were happening in and around my life, and I was not the cause. I spontaneously answered, "Not I-Not I," in response to questions about my insights and abilities.

As noted, Santji also said that, as well as "Neti neti," not this, not that.

Vishwa means universal. *Dharma* means law, religion, or teaching. The word *Zen* points to pure meditation without thought of gain or profit *(musutoku)* and to the activity that is an outgrowth of that practice. If something is universal, it is true. That truth is not dependent on anyone recognizing it as such, but only those who yield their ego, thus expanding their consciousness to receive, will recognize its validity for themselves. There are those who believe that Zen is nontheistic, if not atheistic. Their view is that one who believes in God cannot practice Zen because Zen emphasizes singleness of mind, and, by their very nature, religions promote dualism between God and man.

I do not pretend to be a scholar. It is not my purpose to overwhelm you with research. I will speak to you, as I am ordained to, from direct experience. I do not deny that my spirituality was shaped in the deep ocean of Christianity from my youth. Although there have been tributary streams from other sources, I can say emphatically that Christianity provided the womb for my spiritual birthing. In my case, the Christian experience and Zen are one. This is Vishwa Dharma (Universal Spiritual Law) at work.

Sadguru Sant Keshavadas said boldly, "God is one, many are His names. Truth is one." The words were new to me, but the message rang clearly through me. It resonated in the silence. A practitioner of Islam, Hinduism, Judaism, or any other religion can follow the stream of Zen to its roots and suddenly find themselves embracing Vishwa Dharma, as well. This is true because the only truth that is, originates from the One Eternal Source. No matter how many bits of understanding a given culture may hoard, no one can stop the flow from coming and spreading abroad.

Words are merely tools like a hammer or a saw. When you have driven the nail and finished sawing, you put the tools aside. Unfortunately, it is hard for us to realize that we are giving words more power than they actually have. Just because the words *Vishwa Dharma Zen* do not originate in the English language is no reason they should be feared. English is a relatively young language that has borrowed many words from other languages.

What is important is what the words indicate. Words can be a map, but there are no maps to places no one has ever been. Whereas no words can take us to the highest realms of awakening, those who have experienced the Light of the Secret Place provide clues for others who would follow. In *Soul to Soul,* the nature of Realized Souls is explored to boost your faith in the wisdom of the Master. Nothing in our Western upbringing prepares us to reach within to the source of our being, so, with noted exceptions, the teacher does not have a solid platform here. The pastor, priest, rabbi, and iman have their place of honor. Where is the place for the roshi/the guru in the heart of the believer?

To free yourself as Soul, you need faith in the teachings. There is a great difference between the teachings gleaned from a book and teachings from a living master. It may help you to know the source of living masters. They are a product of an unbroken lineage that bridges time, space, life, and death. The link is soul to soul. If you really understood, the quest for realization would be your happy pursuit day after day.

I believe it was the Zen master Katagiri Roshi who said, "Everything I say is true; if it were not so, I could not teach others." A master is poised to help you achieve enlightenment. Every word and action is expressed for that purpose.

I am but an instrument. The words and empty spaces on these pages come straight from the Source to your soul. Don't stop them in your mind, just let them pass through, and they will do their work in the secret place of your being. If I say, "I can knock the moon out of orbit with the wind generated by a single punch," get flood insurance. There is a flood coming. Your usual mind will dismiss my statement as an idle and meaningless boast. Look deeper. There is something going on you do not see. The Buddha is not smiling for nothing.

III

A Vishwa Dharma Zen Lesson: Zen Mind Is Not Just for Buddhists

There was a time, an eternity ago, when my quest to embrace the Way was a secret quest. I was alone in my experimentation, aware only that I was being guided to step into the unknown with certainty. Since no one knew what I was doing, there was no one to criticize my approach. My intuition, faith, and Scriptures were my only companions along the mysterious path.

There is always something mysterious about the Way; whether it is called the "Do" of Aikido or Karate-do, the Tao, or simply religion, the essence of the spiritual path is the dynamic Unknown. The means by which we attain this path beyond mind is called the Way by many seekers of truth.

Jesus Christ declared, "I am The Way, the truth and the life . . . no man comes unto The Father [The Supreme Mystery] but by me."

The Bible gives us a clue to the inner meaning of this statement. The first verse of the Gospel of John reads: "In the beginning was the Word."

A few sentences down it reads: ". . . and the Word became flesh and came and dwelt among men . . ."

The Word and Jesus Christ are not two. The Word and the Way are one.

Through the ages, the Word moves and speaks through vehicles God chooses or calls for that purpose. When the mind returns to its Original Nature, our actions are naturally spiritual without any need for external or "learned" means. There is a vast difference between teaching the Way and living the Way. I have found that teaching, by its very nature, evokes dualism in the mind, if only temporarily. This phenomenon creates a "catch-22" for the teacher, a glaring contradiction that both student and master must overcome.

Many times people question how I can be both a Christian and a Zen master. The question presupposes that there is a contradiction. The real problem is that people forget that the experience we call spiritual cannot be defined or limited as we can define and limit that which is called religion. Religion has a dogmatic and historical framework, whereas the spiritual path leads to the realization of the beginning-less and indefinable nature of being. We approach religion with our mind. Yet inherent in the study of religion is the impetus to reach far beyond our intellectual capacity to connect with that which the mind can never comprehend or wrap itself around. It is here where most worshippers fail the test.

Strictly religious people never progress beyond the study of the written word to unite with the Living Word, which preceded the Book, whether we are referring to the Bible of Christians, the Koran of Muslims, or any book deemed a Holy Writ. Perhaps those who approach God exclusively through written notes think that it is impossible to connect with the Author in person. Yet the purpose of Scriptures is to lead to the transformation that restores the reader and worshipper to the original living link to the Divine Presence. When a Christian accepts Christ as savior, it is proof that the pure essence of the Word can be received person to person. Christians are familiar with the admonition to become "living epistles," living Scriptures. This is not a command to become a walking tape recorder of the King James Version, a person able to quote any Scripture at will. If we would live by the spirit of the Scriptures, however, our lives would reflect the Way as a matter of course, without effort or conscious design.

The Way did not create religion. The Way is a means of transformation and redemption for mankind, one person at a time. Mankind creates religion as a tool for rediscovering its spiritual roots. We have arbitrarily bound ourselves by attempting to confine the Endless Mystery of God to a comfortable framework for our minds. The Spirit restores man to wholeness. Religion, like the ego-mind, divides. Religion is a function of people. Spirituality is the light of an individual, the son or daughter of God.

In Japanese, another language God speaks, there are the words *joriki* and *tariki*. *Joriki* refers to inner power and *tariki* to outer power.

Zen is usually associated with inner power, thus, traditionally, Zen study does not include mention of "other" power or God. In itself, this is not a cause for alarm if you believe in God. It is a matter of specialization. Tariki, on the other hand, draws its strength from faith in other power, that is, God. Joriki is akin to what Jesus points to as the Kingdom of Heaven, which is within man; the Kingdom of God as an objectified destination is tariki, or other-directed. Whereas Christianity, like Islam, underscores God as the focus for the efforts of believers, the Scriptures also point to an inner path. For example, the Bible tells those who embrace Jesus Christ that the disciple or saint can also "let this mind which was also in Christ Jesus be in you."

Experiencing the same mind as Christ would transform anyone from a secondary position of faith to oneness with the Father (the Supreme). That person would instantly enjoy the same perception of reality as Jesus. This view is verified by the teachings of Christ who said, "I and the Father are one. I would ye be one as we are one." But the religious mind cannot pass through this barrier. It is what is known in Zen as a koan, a spiritual puzzle for the mind. To solve it is to break free of the dilemma. The Prophet Muhammad is a barrier to orthodox Muslims; Buddha is a barrier to most Buddhists; and Jesus Christ, as perceived by the average believer, stands between the disciple and the highest goal he, Jesus, outlined as their birthright: "The disciple cannot be greater than his master but he can be *like* the master" [italics mine].

These barriers are only in the mind.

The mind is like a door that swings two ways. You may use it to go within or to go outside. Lao Tzu taught that, "The Tao is a way of return." If you go within, your journey is not complete until you return to "the marketplace with bliss-bestowing hands," Zen masters say. You must return to your starting place. "Go ye therefore into the world, teaching and preaching whatsoever I have taught you," Jesus said.

It is not the nature of the Way to escape. The fulfillment of man is not in escaping into heaven but in making a round-trip. Our work is right here in the world where we first found ourselves, tilling the soil, screaming over a touchdown, shouting hallelujah on Monday morning. Zen is a prescription for the mind of man.

A clean window casts only shadows when covered by a shade or curtain. If you have a brand-new computer with Windows 95 as the operating system, you will not get Windows XP capability, even if you just took a new computer from the box. Although your spirit may be quickened and redeemed by your faith in the Lord, your mind will still see the world according to its past programming unless it, too, receives a spiritual upgrade. You will experience a greater dichotomy between right and wrong, good and evil, but this will in no way help you defeat the disease Jesus diagnosed as a double-mind. Now you are more deeply torn mentally than ever before. How do you escape this dilemma?

It is this very affliction that is treated by Zen when practiced as joriki, self power. The focus of that practice produces the powerful concentration (samadhi) needed to explore a great mystery. WHAT IS MAN? WHAT AM I? No words will be sufficient to answer these questions. If the Christian believes man is created in the likeness of God, it will forever remain just a belief, though perhaps there will be a faint "race memory" of that age. Something is missing. What is missing is BEING that likeness, not believing in it.

The Zen practitioner hears the same message and plunges into the abyss on a mission that will not cease until he is the manifestation of that likeness. "What is Man that thou art mindful of him?" Speak, if you can. "What is the Son of Man that thou visiteth him?" If you probe with words, the answer will elude you all of eternity. The Way of Zen is direct. If you would be the Son of Man, you must first slay the man in the mirror. Truly, "there can be only one," to borrow the catchphrase from *Highlander,* the popular movie and television series about immortal warriors who fought to be the last warrior standing. Only the surviving warrior will possess the wisdom and power of all others. When you truly understand, son of man, God will visit you.

The conflicts we hear about in the world today are not just the results of those who claim no God, but often the opposite. Many conflicts arise between those who interpret God differently. They are willing to destroy each other because of those perceived differences. Man has always been fighting over his perceptions of what God wants. He has expressed jealousy and rage when others differed in their view of the Author of Life and Creation. In Christianity, we cite the story of Cain and Abel, two brothers who offered God very different gifts. Abel gave a sacrifice that pleased God. Cain did not. Rather than learn from his error, he killed his brother and became the first murderer. Such conflicts have less to do with God than with our misunderstanding of what is being asked of us.

The mind is not ordained to be the teacher of our spirit. What we *think* is of no value in awakening us spiritually. The mind should be an instrument. When we are in proper balance, we do not have mind consciousness. If we are well, we do not feel our internal organs or our skin. They function as if they are not there. Only when there is disease or disorder, do we focus on a finger, our stomach, or whichever part is hurting. When we are in harmony, we are not aware of a mind. It just functions. When a mind is aware of itself, it is proof that it has fallen into duality. Part of its function is to monitor itself. The mind is turned on itself. Since mind is originally empty, just what is our mind obsessed with?

To learn what you are, you must be willing to submit and trust the *upaya* (skillful means) of the teacher. Ordinary means will not do. What is Man? What are you? Forget anthropology, biology, and medical explanations. The Zen way of knowing, the direct way, is to work on your mind. Cultivate *shoshin,* beginner's mind. We should maintain beginner's mind, as the late Master Shunryu Suzuki taught. That is a great lesson to practice. Maintain beginner's mind.

You may have felt something within you leap when you came in contact with the teachings for the first time. If this is so, it is this *something* within you that must be allowed to flower.

A roshi or guru can only water a seed and cast light on it. He does not choose the plant or flower you will become; the answer is locked within the seed itself. Unlike the seeds of the plant kingdom, which produce millions of clones, the seed within you produces a one-of-a-kind, never-before-seen plant . . . and no one will ever see it unless you allow it to blossom.

This single seed in you is the one thought (*nen* in Japanese). This consciousness I refer to is the primordial self before the birth of your mother and father, so I am not speaking of your body nor of the memories you think are you. Like all who are born on this planet, you have become so thoroughly identified with form and thought that you are unable to experience the deeper aspects of LIFE. If a single thought (nen) is you, what happens when that one thought is divided?

Zen is living in the immediacy of an experience, direct contact with life at its source without hesitation, deliberation, or conscious effort. It is acting with the totality of our being with nothing left over or held back. This is impossible to achieve with a double-mind, a mind attempting to monitor or control an experience while it is taking place.

The spiritual path, which the word *Zen* indicates, does not depend on logic for its success. I underscore this despite the fact that we are able to use logic to illustrate points about Zen after we have a great satori. This ability to point to things beyond the reach of intellect using constructs from the mind is not just the hallmark of Zen Buddhist literature. Jesus spoke in parables to illustrate spiritual truths and gurus tell elaborate stories to illuminate the minds of their students.

Christianity, Zen, the martial arts are a seamless thread to me. There is no need for me to divide myself. There are contradictions only when we harbor the need to examine everything using the medium of words. Once again, I am reminded of the words of Sant Keshavadas, "Neti neti—not this, not that." To have attachment to labels is to disrupt the flow of life-giving Spirit by constructing conscious barriers to impede the natural flow. Labels are what other beings use in their attempt to "comprehend" your actions. If you fall prey to this practice yourself, you will block enlightenment. If you have read this far, you are being drawn to the inner path, the Kingdom of Heaven. This is the Original Home of *Adam,* which is Hebrew for "Man." It has always been here within you. It has always been accessible. Deception and ignorance blind us to it. The Light is within and without.

> The Light shineth in the darkness but the
> darkness comprehendeth it not.
>
> —The Gospel of John

> I am the light of the world . . .
>
> —Jesus Christ

As long as you remain apart from the Light Within your mind, it is impersonal. The reference to the Christ as the Light of the World demonstrates that when one comprehends that Light, he becomes the personification of the Light. It is written in the Gospel of John that "The Word became flesh and came and dwelt among men." This is further confirmation that it is possible for the object of meditation and worship to become one with the worshipper or devotee. Only when this is the truth of your actual experience, only when you realize this infusion of Light for yourself, can you say without hesitation or doubt these words attributed to the Buddha:

> In the heavens above, in the earth below,
> I, alone, am the most honored one.

It may shock many people that I speak of Zen using the Bible as a reference more than I do any other source. It is an absolute must that I am true to my own experience. I was born to the practice of Dhyana (Zen) before I knew of such a path. I was consciously raised in and found my spiritual life through Christ. Since my spiritual connection was a living one brought to life by my childhood personal encounter with the Living Christ, the profound nature of this darshan (vision of the Lord), not dogma, became the foundation of my spiritual strength. On my birthday, one of my students, Jon Zuck, expressed the essence of how I view the relationship between Christ and Buddha. His painting, created without input from me, was a blessing. It depicted Jesus Christ touching the brow center of Buddha as he sat under the Bo tree. The disciples of both Jesus and Buddha are lined up in the distance. Satori did not erase my relationship or understanding of Jesus Christ. It deepened the experience. Another time, my students Moses McFarland and Sean Engle gave me a blue samurai sword. Sadguru Sant Keshavadas often called me "The Blue One," for Krishna. The color had meaning to me. Krishna is said to be the destroyer of demons. In his free time, however, he is depicted as a playful and loving (read roguish) incarnation of God.

Secure in my faith in the Supreme Lord, the mind became my lifelong study. By age 19, I was ripe to meet Zen master Nomura Roshi and primed to absorb lightning-bolt teachings in a flash. When I encountered Sadguru Sant Keshavadas ten years later, he proceeded to prepare me for my mission. He made several things clear. There was no need for me to alter my Zen approach to practice, nor deny my Christian heritage. I accepted Nomura Roshi, Sadguru Sant Keshavadas, and all the spiritual personages who ever blessed my life as extensions of my original darshan with Christ. I extended this humble acceptance of teachers and supporters not only to those who appeared to me in flesh and blood, but also recognized that all saints, sages, prophets, and spiritual warriors of the past, present, and future are manifestations of the Single Mind/ Universal Spirit of the Cosmos. Without a religious mind to block the avenues of revelation, truth can be sipped from many vessels. God is one. The lover of the Divine can find his Beloved no matter what disguise is worn. "Try the spirit by the spirit to see, if it be of God," the Scriptures warn. To do this, we must learn to measure things with our spirits, not our minds. But how?

Gurus appear in every culture and religion. There is no need for a guru to denounce his culture or native religion to do his work. By staying where he is, a guru can expand the vision of his people and still reach out to everyone who comes to him. A guru may be born to a particular religion but he belongs to no religion. He is an emissary of God. His body is born of flesh, but inwardly he is born of the Spirit . . . Unborn. He is like Melchizedek, with no beginning or end of life . . . Tathagatha, in Sanskrit, a being who comes and goes without a trace. A guru is a being God causes to be in the world to dispel darkness from the mind of humanity. In effect, the guru is a personification of God's Mind, Cosmic Mind, Buddha Mind, call it what you will. When you sit before the guru, you are in the presence of that Spiritual Mind. Wisdom, radiant emptiness, life beyond form or phenomenon reveals itself moment by moment through the person and personality of the one who is called guru, when you humble yourself and sit at his feet.

In a few simple words, but more explicitly by his actions, Sant Keshavadas outlined the nature of gurus, my nature. I should teach and speak only what comes unimpeded from the Source of Being. The chosen teachers are spiritual emissaries sent to shed light on the condition of humanity, not to court favor by seeking agreement with the mind. To speak and act from this traceless source is what is indicated by the word *Zen*.

The grasping mind of man always seeks to define things and people as well. Yet, you, the student of the Way, must not harbor definitions. Definitions are only expression in words, but they bind your mind. You must also go beyond techniques; they are frozen movements without life. If you want to live life as it bubbles up from the fountain, you must stop clinging to words and ideas and drink life as it comes.

From the strict standpoint of religion, the world would see Sant Keshavadas as a Hindu. He was never Hindu with me. For more than 20 years, I yielded to his guidance and all I experienced was the Wind of the Spirit blowing through a human vessel. This was his example to me. Throughout those years, I went to church even when I lived in the temple. I practiced Zen and martial arts and read my Bible with only encouragement from the master . . . and the cosmic path became clearer.

I did not meditate to become a Buddhist or Hindu or even a better Christian. It was simpler than that. My spirit demanded that I turn my mind to the silence within. It was a delicious longing, but no place was indicated. I just knew without knowing that home was not what I saw with my eyes. As far as I was concerned, this was a private matter that involved no one but me. Strange how the world fights to destroy our access to our own soul. What does the world fear? How does it block us?

You must enter the path from where you are. Where are your feet right now?

Though I never doubted the existence of God, I did have problems with people who seemed to delight in speaking as if He was something finite, as if there was some virtue in putting him in a category. I accepted the mission and person of Jesus Christ, but I did not focus my faith in what other people said. I sat at the feet of the Master myself. Time and space are only barriers to the physical being, not the spiritual being.

In my parents' home, God was approached according to the Christian path, so I started right there. My outer path was clearly Christianity. Jesus meditated and sought renewal in moments of silence and solitude; so did I. As I matured spiritually, I realized that, although Christians could see and believe in Jesus as Lord, they overlooked the foundation of his mission. He was first an enlightened human being.

Had Jesus lived a little farther east, his title could have been Buddha.

It was clear to me that Jesus was a realized soul before he was called "the Son of God," before he was Christed at the Baptismal under the hand of John "the Baptist."

This is an important clue in unraveling the secret that will set you free.

You may have a limited view of Jesus if you are not a Christian, but it is even more likely that your view of him is limited if you *are* a Christian. The Zen of the guru deals only with living truth and living masters. The network that connects one master to another is called lineage. The line of communion with the ultimate has not been disconnected, nor has the line of communion with the finite (humanity). If you seek it, you can find the truth. If you limit your search to what is advertised on television, in publications, and in the Yellow Pages, you may miss the Real.

Though salvation or restoration to the Spirit of God is freely given to those who ask for it, enlightenment is not a gift. As a little boy, I began the quest for enlightenment, although I did not verbalize the hunger of my "way-seeking mind." The moment that quest began I went off the radar of the church. The church promotes and provides maintenance for the "saved." Enlightenment is not on its agenda. God did not assign that work to the church.

To some he sent preachers. To others he sent teachers. How can they hear without a preacher? How can they learn without a teacher?

People can hear a preacher. They can repeat what they hear and memorize it. The work of a teacher is largely done in the spirit. It is passed on without words. Who can comprehend that? In that context, this statement about the Buddha may be clear:

The Buddha preached for more than 49 years but never spoke a word.

In my experience, the teacher does not educate the mind; he helps us defeat it so that it can be brought under the authority of the Spirit. The student of the Way is a spiritual warrior not a sheep. He faces the greatest battle there is: the battle over the world-trained mind.

If you can remember this one thing, then you will know why you need not worry about what others think of your path to realization . . . *they think*. When you are called to this path, your steps are ordered by Heaven's will, not by your own. You need only refer to the deep movement within you about which no one but you knows. Trust this alone.

You can only get there from where you are. If the nontheistic Zen approach worked for you, you would not be here. If dedication to church service was all you needed, you would not be here. If your devotion to the way of the warrior fed the hunger of your soul, you would not be reading this. You are a person who needs a holistic message . . . but you already feel the truth of it.

Do not analyze these lessons, do not block, just sip from this word tea and smell its aroma. Then leave your computer and do what you will. There is garbage in the can. Take it out. Play with the children; caress your spouse. Take a walk.

It is with you in all these activities, but don't seek it in thought. If you do, it will flee as far way away as the other side of the universe.

I like this mantra.

GOD IS . . .

It is matched by a different yet equal realization without equivocation . . .

I AM . . .

You are the only one reading this. Which of these statements is the absolute TRUTH?

There is plenty of religious talk about peace and love, but it's very hard to see the evidence in day-to-day life. It is popular to quote Zen writings these days. The ancient masters wrote sparkling treasures, but where is the Zen writing today? None can be written to illuminate the darkness without genuine enlightenment. There can be no realization until there is no "you" left to recognize the process. Jesus said, "Take no thought!" There is no truer Zen instruction than that. Buddha was not a Buddhist. He was Siddhartha Gautama. Jesus was not a Christian. He was Jesus of Nazareth. When thoughts fall away, there is no designation left. Just this . . . No Thought . . . No Mind, which is what we mean by Zen. Zen is like lightning. By the time you formulate your mouth to say the word . . . it is gone.

When Christ appeared to me when I was nine, there was no instruction given. He looked into my eyes and I understood. The first time I spoke, I fell headlong from grace. If you have read this far, you need to remember but this: Chew words, swallow them, digest them, then head for the nearest toilet and sit. By the time they flush out the other end, you will be right where you need to be to learn.

When I stood outside New Calvary Baptist Church with Sadguru

Sant Keshavadas, circa 1982, he reflected on the words he had just spoken to members of the black community. Reverend Milton "the Disciple" Reid, a well-known civil rights activist and friend of Dr. Martin Luther King Jr., had permitted the guru to speak in the education wing of the church. "I can only go but so far," he said. "I am from Asia. They cannot understand me, but they can understand you. Teach your people to harness the power of the Mind. They are the most spiritual people in the world, but they do not understand the Mind. Teach them to harness it and they can have anything they want on this Earth."

Santji always spoke to me as an equal. His tone of voice and delivery told me he clearly expected me to rise and meet any challenge set before me. The path is universal. God is one. Santji was telling me that God wanted to fix the African-American Mind; he needed an African American for the job.

This was a koan the Guru had given me. How could one man possibly spin the mind-set of millions of people? Was there a black Universal Mind, an African-American Zen to teach? My love for people knows no racial distinction, but that did not mean that I was not aware that a problem existed. Race has always been a factor in the world I knew. In that moment, Guruji altered my practice. There was the koan, a mystery to solve that would transform my life and take me and others to hitherto unknown regions of joy and power.

The question took shape. The universe has a sly sense of humor. The universe plays with words. The question, the barrier to be passed, formed as this: WHAT IS THE SOUND OF ONE BLACK HAND CLAPPING?

The fate of the Earth, the healing of your world, depends on the solution. You have a vested interest in probing the question yourself. No matter what culture you claim as yours, the black hand you do not see or recognize has you trapped. No one can answer this koan for you. You must take it within your mind. We will meditate on that a little more as we proceed.

The Buddha said, "In the heavens above and the earth below, I alone am the most honored one . . ."

Hmmm.

Reaching within, I tap the vibrant stream that is the spirit of my fathers, my ancestors. Shakyamuni Buddha is Indian. I am clear now. If

I believe his declaration as the final word, that it applied only to Shakyamuni Buddha himself, I would have to accept that my African ancestors, the spirit and mind of my soul are inconsequential in the scheme of the universe. There can be only one, after all. Then I learn he wants to be my friend. He wants to go home with me. I bow. That Buddha is full of bull. Now let's get serious and examine the real issue.

IV

Black Hand Clapping! "Who Is the Master?"

For a brief time in my childhood, the world was without limitation. I could go wherever my mind could soar. My mind soared in and out of many dimensions. Gradually, my world became smaller, not because I lacked the power to continue my spiritual flights, but because it became necessary to protect the vulnerable part, to protect my bodily life and well-being from outside threats. There were influences close to home, but the biggest shock and most repressive of all the things I learned in the early years was: I was not a person; I was black.

From the moment I learned that the mere color of my skin gave others the feeling I could be disrespected, restricted, ignored, and otherwise abused, I was determined not to accept the distortion. Though it seemed clear from what I learned in school that it was the practice of my country to discriminate between one color of human and another, even as a child I could not accept it. I knew that there was something fundamentally wrong with doing that to others, and there was something fundamentally wrong with the persons who allowed it to happen. I became a student of other cultures. Since it appeared that the men of my own community were not resisting this soul-destroying outrage, I did not see a suitable role model to guide me to true manhood. I needed to learn about the real nature of men since those around me were being obedient to a decree designed to keep them in bondage. I also looked at my own skin differently for the first time.

Before the realization that my people had been slaves, I did not understand why so much emphasis was placed within our community on complexion. Long before I knew of a racial divide or even that there was such a designation as race, I heard people around me remark on the "shade" of a person's skin. When I used the word "me," as a child, it was all-inclusive; my awareness of self did not factor in my skin color. Spirit permeates everything. It radiates everywhere. It is not impeded by material objects, or anything else. I was to discover, however, through day-to-day experience, that the mind can block the spirit. This was long before I ever came across the biblical warning that, "The mind and the spirit are enmity to each other." The mind and the spirit are in conflict. This is the disorder. It can be treated.

A person of any culture who seeks the path of Self-Realization is seeking the path that reveals the truth of original nature. That being transcends time and place. It is a path driven by faith not logic. Logic draws on what is known and what can be proven. The logical may be accessible to the senses and observable by the mind. Yet to explore one's essential nature is to connect with the essence of one's life, that which is the fundamental stuff of one's being before the advent of birth and before the first thought has formed. While it may seem a very mystical way of saying it, mind cannot comprehend Mind. Yet this same point is made in the Bible: "The ways of God are high above the ways of Man." (God is The Mind of the Universe, as much as He is The Spirit of the Universe.) Christianity teaches that man is created in the likeness of God. Using this model, we can see that man is meant to be a reflection of God's nature. From this view we can determine the problem. God's Mind and Spirit, all aspects of God, work in harmony. Various aspects of our nature are in conflict. It is because of this schism between spirit and mind that the mind can throw up roadblocks that impede spirit.

In the 1950s, it was not uncommon for even a parent to lay the groundwork for the formulation of the skin barrier. The spirit is affected when a child hears the words, "Stay out of the sun, you're getting too dark" or "Your hair is so kinky, you have bad hair," or hears people with lighter skin described as beautiful, while darker people are spoken of in a manner significantly different: "She would be beautiful, if she wasn't so dark." The message being sent is that you do not fit the positive standard. You become self-conscious. To be self-conscious is to stop the flow or hesitate to act. The Zen admonition "Above all don't wobble" addresses this malaise. To be uncertain about how to proceed or to hold back artificially is a consciousness flaw. Other people may attempt to stop us from acting on our freedom through physical might or intimidation of another sort, but nothing is more effective than our internalization of "the code" that binds us. Once we have internalized these codes, we block ourselves.

If we are just ourselves, there is no concept to contend with. When flesh and its coloration, height, and weight become the factors used to judge us, we are bound to a fixed form and a locked-down definition. So as history, media, and literature all established the white ideal as the ideal for all, consciously and unconsciously the minds of the governed measure the person against the standard. Conformity, assimilation to whatever degree possible, becomes a delusion of acceptance. The logical mind says, "If we conform, they will see we are just like them and treat us better." Even if this were so, it would be a problem. The Others would accept you, but you would reject yourself. If you were taught that because you are white, you are better than other people, taught that you belong on a pedestal, you are believing a lie also.

These lies that bind us to our skin diminish our lives. A man can enjoy power and material wealth for a season, but mansions on earth crumble before the moment of death. The treasure of the soul shines all the brighter at that moment. Death is but a transition . . . throw the switch . . . pow! There is light. While the Realized Soul is not fazed by death, the beauty of his work and his being is that he is free to exercise spirit on earth. He is a living spirit, not a living body. This is a major point. Those who have manipulated mankind to concentrate on the politics of skin and other superficialities are "demons."

The gods of this world care only for themselves. To play white against black, to divide all the beautiful people because they look or talk differently, ignores that we all have but a single origin.

There is a universal need for "liberation" because all human beings are bound in some way, though we are not bound in the same way. On the surface, it would appear that some classes of people have no chains on them at all. While they may have fewer social and economic restrictions, even these people are bound by invisible cords. Money and position free "successful" African Americans to move more freely in society, but they cannot break the bond fashioned of skin. Since this bond is created by thought, they remain unliberated, even though they stand about in Gucci shoes and lean against their Ferraris. Despite money and prestige, as long as there is a split in the mind, there remains something that keeps them apart from the whole. As long as there is a conscious need to assert one's difference, there is a lack of fluidity in the spirit.

There is nothing wrong with expressing the uniqueness inherent in different cultures, but these expressions should arise as a matter of course, not out of any self-conscious need to prove something to others. Culture arises naturally from a people, like exhalations flow naturally from inhalations. Culture is the natural manifestation of the human spirit. Others may feel a need to qualify or define us and some people may seek to confine us to a limited role because they perceive us as different from themselves, but we must never create a conceptual trap for ourselves.

I walked away from school knowing that I was not an American but a member of a perpetual underclass. The world did not feel the same to me. My father taught me to revere the flag. He was a Cub Scout leader, and he supported our graduation to the Boy Scouts. We were an American family. Now I was supposed to accept that others had sway over my life because my skin color was not acceptable to the larger society. I felt betrayed and angry. If this was the truth, it seared me. I was only in the fourth grade. I was powerless to do anything about the world around me—but a fire ignited within. I knew I could not accept the conditions of arbitrary external controls on my life. Such thoughts went against all I had been taught. I was already alive as a soul. I decided I would let no one bury me alive.

In church, I learned how God saw me. I did not understand why people who believed the words in the Bible could mistreat other humans or how those who read about David and Goliath failed to call on God to defeat the Goliath in their lives.

In Zen, it is not Zen to just believe. I did not feel that any other person was superior to me, thus free to rule my life. Anger is a good thing. The angry soul will not let the interloper in to do his work. You must work on yourself. If you were not white, black, red, yellow, brown, or purple, and no one else was divided in that manner either, how would you experience yourself?

Practice

Give no one you meet on the road this week any special treatment. Treat everyone as if there is no race, just a diversity of personalities.

Know O Israel, the Lord thy God is One, He has created all nations of one blood.

You have a large family; throw open the East Gate, West Gate, South Gate, and North Gate and greet your six billion siblings.

"It is time to teach the world to sing in perfect harmony." Coca-Cola was right—we really can teach the world to sing.

V

Crossing Paths

Until I was 12, I grew up in a somewhat sheltered world that provided a belief system that bound people, hand, foot, and mind to the gods of this world, while paying homage to the Lord of Heaven. From earliest childhood, my parents established that the power of and behind the universe, the source of its creation and all within it, was a being we called God. Although the word "God" was used to designate His existence, it was made clear that God Himself defied definition. He is, it was said, omniscient, omnipresent, and omnipotent. "In Him we move and have our being."

The most fascinating comment about God to me was that He is without beginning or end. I tried to wrap my mind around and probe that statement: no beginning—no end? How could anything or anyone exist that did not first come into being? In Zen parlance, "No beginning" became my first koan, a psychospiritual barrier to break through. While pondering that koan, one thing was certain to me, and in that one thing my faith rested. My existence was not rooted in what I could see, but in the being I learned to call God. I was not seeking to find Him or to question Him, I felt the longing to let go and merge with Him. This yearning came early in my life.

It is important to clarify here that belief in God is not a weakness. The weakness lies in the binding (mostly through religious dogma) that men wrap around the Peerless Creator. Religion comes from the Latin root word *religare,* which means "to bind" . . . and so it does. The forms men slap on the formless guide the mind down a corridor, blinding it to the vastness of the One they worship. The forms also serve to limit their spiritual advancement to that which can be defined or observed by other men.

This quiet and tacit understanding that God was not to be found in thoughts was no doubt aided by my intuitive attraction to seated meditation and the presence of strong samadhi (concentration). Of course, being an African-American youth, raised in the Southern Baptist church, I had no vocabulary to describe my behavior and my parents only labeled it as peculiar. My mother first noticed that I was prone from the age of three years old to sit motionless and slip into an altered state. She would find me sitting up in my bed in the wee hours of the morning in the dark, staring into the void, my eyes seemingly shining, she told me. I continued the practice through the years. In 1967, a Japanese Buddhist monk, the Zen master Nomura Roshi, revealed that I was practicing the Zen method of meditation called *shikantaza* (just sitting). His revelation opened the gate for my hitherto unconscious practice to move into a new dimension. The spiritual deepening process, a by-product of meditation, gave me a strong sense of God's presence.

There is a difference between God as invoked in church service and the Presence, which was the profound oneness growing out of my meditation. The God of church is experienced psychologically as external, apart from the worshipper in a discernible way. The God of my meditation permeates my being and all the universe. There is no separation. It is God within who empowers and frees our minds. As I ponder the role of the modern church and examine the history of Africans in America, along with that of other members of America's so-called minorities, I see that there is a vision that not only separates them from the God they worship, but also from the Original Mind itself. Poised between them and the spirit is flesh and blood, not just their own, which is barrier enough, but also the flesh and blood of countless others.

Perhaps it is because I had already begun to probe the depths of my soul life that I became incensed at the thought that someone other than I expected pivotal control of my life and actions. I paid attention in

Sunday school. I was taught that "Man was given dominion over the Earth." The decree did not designate a particular color of man, but mankind, as in the plural sense. Was I to believe that this Scripture was a lie? I had a choice. Either I believed the spiritual teachings that spoke of power and grace or yielded to the sociopolitical forces that brought my people to their knees in psychological defeat. I made my choice. There is a universal truth. There is an immutable essence of man. I was to discover that "the Supreme Lord," the Divine Presence, is too big to be encompassed or owned by any religion or confined to a particular hemisphere. God is working out the koan called Man. As has been pointed out through the ages, God, the Universal, operates through the medium of a surrendered mind. There are some missions that can only be accomplished by those who have the power to act on faith. Only faith-powered action carries the divine signature.

The God of this world is like a master chess player who easily defeats those who come to the board with only their intellect. He plays by spirit. Those who come to the field of battle in the Name, that is, in the spirit of the Supreme, are responsive to His will. They are able to move in subtle and unpredictable ways because their mind is the Original Mind of Man, No-Mind. No-Mind is a perfect conduit for the Spirit of the Universe. All of these terms point to the same thing. By design, the human being is meant to be a reflection of the nature of his creator. He should function effortlessly, without internal conflict, to perform his work and achieve his goals. When the communion between mind and spirit in the medium of the body is broken, the worldview becomes distorted.

While wounds inflicted on the human soul are tragically personal, even something so personal can be a metaphor. In fact, studying the personal impact of a problem is helpful in understanding larger issues. It has become common to discount the individual, as if a greater number can magically exist without the formula one plus one. This is not so. As you will come to see, the soul of man is "one." What is done to "one body" affects the soul of "every body." As a child, I would hear the old folks say, "What goes around comes around." Later, when I had a deeper understanding of the philosophies of the world, I recognized that they were speaking of what Buddhists and Hindus call karma. Our actions create cause and effect, and the scale will be balanced one day.

On any Sunday morning, the hymns in the African-American church are sung to a mighty backdrop of handclapping and foot-stomping. As a child, I felt that the men and women in church constituted an awesome army who could push back any enemy. Listening to that sound and feeling the power inherent in their holy clapping and foot-stomping made me feel secure. I believed in these "soldiers of the cross." Later, I would come to associate "old-time religion" with Bhakti Yoga, the path of uniting with God through worship. Karma is not a respecter of time or person. In the distance, I feel the presence of my ancestors. Black Hand is clapping on both sides of the river. On the surface, the offspring of Africa do not know about the power escaping from their soul, just as ancestors of those who have built their kingdoms on bloodshed and suffering may not be aware of their soul debt. There is an accounting coming. Whether it is destructive or healing can still be decided—but only today. Where do you stand, today?

VI

What Is Man?

The question, "What is man?" is not a philosophical one to wrestle with in thought. It is a trigger for realizing a simple truth. I will repose the question with a slight change. What are you? Now, if I snatch all the elements of your mind away—cognition, consciousness, short and long-term memory, the unconscious, everything—who are you then? Can you answer? Are you still present?

Man is fundamentally the Mind. We live through the medium of Mind. On the basic level, the mind points back to our own bodies and souls. It feeds information and experiences that formulate our sensation of life as lived in our individual bodies. Those with higher awareness include other lives in their field of awareness. They know that what they are capable of feeling is also within the realm of probability for others. When such a person misses stepping on a nail, he will remove it from the path of others because he does not want them to feel its sharp bite either. This person is his brother's keeper. There is both an inflow and outflow to his consciousness. In some people, these two natures function as one.

It is because it is possible to extend our awareness and concern beyond our own bodies that there is hope that greater consciousness of the human condition can be raised. The journey to correct the self-centered and destructive flaw in the human condition started thousands of years ago. We are accustomed to viewing the shortcomings of society in terms of politics and social issues. We forget or fail to see that the crux of our problem lies in our own spiritual condition and misuse of this power we call the mind.

The question "What is man?" is not different from the Zen koan "What is the sound of one hand clapping?" An intellectual response to either question is not enough. I have suggested that man is essentially mind, but that leaves you with an even greater mystery. What is mind? The journey we need to take is not one of thought. It is thought that entangled us in the first place. We do not need to have words about ourselves. We need to BE ourselves. We do not need to be able to write a discourse on the mind, we need to function from Original Mind. Buddhists, Hindus, and practitioners of Higher Yoga, Taoism, and related studies coming out of Asia study the mind as a matter of course, but they are not exclusive. I grew from Christian spiritual soil. After my satori, I could clearly see the Zen teachings on the mind evident throughout the Bible. It was clear that the ultimate teachings belonged to no one and to all. Discernment is necessary to understanding.

Four hundred years ago, there was a conspiracy to destroy the African and make of him something less than human. In this age of high technology and amazing accomplishments, the problem of human consciousness remains. It is still common for the government to address citizens in racial terms. Though there are the privileged and the underprivileged, the belief that there is truly a black American and a white American is false. The American Consciousness is a composite of many cultures. If some Caucasians still believe themselves to be the sole personification of that spirit, they are wrong.

There is but one mind at work in the universe and it must, by nature, seek and restore its own balance and harmony. It is always seeking the means to carry out its mission. Like the Spirit of God, Universal Mind also employs human agents to fulfill its mission. Sadguru Sant Keshavadas liked the term "Cosmic Mind." Whatever deed is performed by the power of Cosmic Mind is directed toward the completion of the ULTIMATE GOAL of our creator. So vast and so awesome is this plan, it is not to be comprehended even by those charged to act by its authority.

The chosen agents of this Divine Mind must be unquestionably true to their own mission. The kind of faith that is necessary to do this mirrors the faith that spiritual activists throughout the ages have had to demonstrate. Only the source of the soul can heal the soul. This is not a political or social journey, although it may seem so on the surface. It has been said countless times that God is one.

Spiritual teachings point to the oneness of mankind, a trait we share with the Lord of the Worlds. One person makes a difference. That is the message of Christ when he said, "If I be lifted up I will draw *all* men unto me" [italics mine].

It was the message of Buddha, amplified by Zen Master Hakuin in his poem "Hakuin Zenji zazen-wasan": "All men are buddhas [potentially enlightened ones]. It is like ice and water. Apart from water no ice can exist. Apart from men there can be no buddhas."

The gaping wound in the soul of the black man cannot be healed by mere religion. While a reservation in heaven is attractive to the spirit of an individual, the crippling disease that retards the healing of the universe and prevents the restoration of divine order cannot be culminated after death. There is work to be done that can only be done in this world in the housing of the body. For this work to be effective, the body of HUMANITY (the body of Christ) must come together as one. This unity cannot be manipulated by diplomacy or any form of intellectual device. When each part of the body (or tribes of humanity) finds its own enlightenment (not each member, but through the vehicle of a type of chosen priest), the union will occur, just as when sunlight hovers over water, the reflection is forthcoming.

It is now the time of Black Hand, a time for the universe to find its African lineage again and come alive as fully Man. It is known that the Holy Spirit flows to each new believer. The Word dwells within the disciple. Yet the saints of old-time religion and most believers born in the Western Hemisphere would fail to understand this: We are also buddhas. In simple terms, Original man enjoyed both the Mind and the Spirit of God. It is the loss of that realization that sent men into despair. The Sanskrit word *Buddha* means to be awake, or "The Awakened One." Without understanding of these Mind teachings or Dharma, there is no way to redeem the mind. It is because both saints and sinners use the mind of delusion, not the Awakened Mind, that the human race remains capable of the most evil deeds, despite their proclaimed faith in a loving God.

The Africans brought to America to perform slave labor were the victims of dualistic mind. While there have been some notable advancements in human relations, dualism still rules. As a result, that which could destroy the America of vision is not the terrorist of the news, but the terror that still lies within us. If you listen well, you can hear the sound of clapping. It is just one hand, one black hand striking nothing in particular. It can save America, if you are receptive to the rhythm of its truth; if not, this one hand thought to belong to an insignificant people may bring the country to its knees. It is inevitable. There are laws. According to the laws of karma, the scales must balance. For centuries, the souls of a people held in bondage, physically, mentally, spiritually, and economically, cried out for justice, or thirsted for revenge. That force was eternalized. Where does it go?

The Fury of Nature

Hurricane Katrina left devastation in the wake of her furious winds. New Orleans, Louisiana, a city known for Mardi Gras and the French Quarter and as a mecca for jazz musicians, was obliterated under high winds and flood waters that drowned hundreds of people and ended the livelihood of those left standing. The question is often asked, "Why did God allow this to happen?"

My answer is that God did not cause the storm. Man is the storm. The mind of man, constantly divided against itself, is an energy field that is out of control. Hit the hardest by Katrina were the poor people. The people who had almost nothing are now completely without.

It has not gone unnoticed that the city of New Orleans has a majority African-American citizen base. The city may be famous, but it has many people within its borders who have been living on the edge of the modern age. When the mind is discontented, especially if the negativity or rage is directed at someone else, it will only grow stronger if ignored. Your mind is not just in your head, it permeates the environment, and affects the world around you. We can feel the mood of another person because that individual is telegraphing it through the ether. Unrest inside of us translates into unrest in our environment. Just as ignorance of the Law is no excuse, ignorance of Dharma does not save you from the effects of forces you choose not to acknowledge. Thoughts can kill. Man was given dominion over the Earth. That means our minds had power over the elements, as well as the living creatures. Suppose that we never lost the power, we just forgot how to control it; we forgot how to maintain awareness and how to protect the environment. We broke off our connection with that part of ourselves, so now we view the evidence of our own confusion as storms.

Anger suppressed today,
Lightning storm
Thunderclaps tonight.

If we could find peace and harmony within, if that state of mind would flow from person to person we would soon have a *sangha* (community) of sorts, which, instead of just talking about it, radiates peace vibrations directly into nature. We would have a measurable effect on the Earth.

This kind of transformation cannot be a publicity stunt. It cannot come about just because it is a good idea. First, people have to realize that there is a volcano of anger within them that has been buried forever. It is poisoning the carrier and the planet. They must be willing to face their fear of the unknown to bring the beast into the open air. There is another kind of fear: the fear of the known.

There may be something that holds you back from expressing the truth of yourself. What do you fear? If you do not face that fear, you may spend your entire life living by a script someone else wrote for you. It will be as if you never lived because, frankly, you do not know what life really is. If your spirit is held a prisoner of the flesh and mind, you are simply sleepwalking. You might as well pull the covers up; you are dreaming you're reading a book.

If you are to come alive as a soul, you must break through the barriers guarded by the bogeyman. The way to freedom leads straight past your fears.

We can learn something from Warrior Zen.

The path of the saint and the way of the warrior are not so different. Both the saint and the warrior face a formidable enemy. The saint must elude the "fiery darts" of Satan, and the warrior faces the human embodiment of death, his mortal enemy.

The secret of Bushido, "The Way of the Warrior," rests on a single pillar: the warrior, the samurai, must be willing to die at any moment. He must, in fact, be determined to die. This point is underscored time and again by D. T. Suzuki, in *Zen and Japanese Culture.* Suzuki introduced Zen to the Western world.

From Trevor Leggett's *Samurai Zen: The Warrior Koans* (Routledge, 2003), the death poem of Zen master Bukko further illustrates the Zen view of death.

> Buddhas and ordinary men are equally illusions.
> If you go looking for the true form, it is a speck of dust in the eye.
> The burnt bones of this old monk embrace heaven and earth.
> Do not scatter the cold ashes to mountain and sky.

Jesus Christ also taught this "Zen" to his disciples. He admonished them that those who attempted to preserve their lives would lose them. Those who gave up their lives would find them.

This theme is definitely universal and not specific to religions. Krishna tells Arjuna to do his duty in battle and that life and death are under the control of the supreme deity, not man.

The reluctant warrior fears pain and the loss of his bodily life under the blows of the enemy's weapon. The fearful saint or monk seeking to embrace the Unknown trembles at the thought of losing his ego. Nothing can be more terrifying for a person who believes that he or she is the ego, the opinionated consciousness, the knowing one, than the thought that this seeing and hearing, thinking and analyzing identity could be lost.

The Inner Master communing through the form of roshi or guru says, "Die to this world, I will meet you on the other side."

Do you believe? Do you believe what Lao Tzu told his disciples when speaking of the Great Way, known as *Tao* in Chinese, "The Tao is a way of return"? If you do, then this is your time to show it, this is your swan song, the poem that precedes your death. The gateway to abundant life admits only the soul of man. Walk with me, but don't dare look back.

> The road is straight ahead into eternity.
> Mind aimed but focusing on nothing that can be seen,
> There is a path arising but no feet to walk it,
> Streaking pass the stars,
> There is music I can only feel not hear,
> The rhythm alone is me.
>
> —Vernon Kitabu Turner

VII

You Are Not Okay

No matter what you believe about the creation of life, whether you hold exclusively to the explanations of science or center your faith in one of the many religious paths that recognize God as the source of all things, there is at least one focus of faith we all believe in: the Mind. Like God, the Mind cannot be seen. Its origin is a mystery, its powers are awesome, its boundary is unknown. There is no human being who does not benefit from the function of the Mind. We cannot go a single day without it, yet its true nature not only escapes the understanding of the most intellectual and gifted of human beings, its power is also underestimated by those who consider themselves students of God.

Even as birds large and small fly through the same sky, and fish and whales swim in the same vast ocean, all human beings of every culture share the Mind. This is not understood. Ignorance of how the Mind works makes you vulnerable to control. Most people are dancing under a string pulled this way and that by forces they never see. Chances are great that you are one of these people. It is said that "ignorance is bliss." If you believe that, it only proves the manipulation point just made. Ignorance hurts. You may have no clue about what you are missing, but you are suffering from the loss anyway.

The Yin-Yang symbol depicts a combination of male and female energies that contain an element of their opposite. Together, the pair of opposites forms more than a combination of the two powers. They create a third power, which is represented by the circle that binds them. Tremendous energy and animosity is expended by people who want to own the truth as if it is private property. When it comes to the nature of our being, truth must be universal and accessible to all, for it is the root of what is hidden within us and waiting to be realized. It is not exclusive to those who speak a certain language or live in a particular locality.

Christianity, proper, does not address the existence of a feminine aspect of God, but the Bible points to it, nonetheless.

In Genesis, God says, "Let us make man in our own image." The passage continues, "In His image created He him, male and female created He them." In the most simple way, God reveals His image, that is, the totality of the Godhead, which includes a feminine side. This is pointed to in a show-and-tell method. The "them" included a male and female spirit in two separate packages. Now meditate on that.

Don't analyze! Meditate on it. Receive it silently, drink it in. Then wait until the nourishing truth takes effect.

I have come to understand that no one person, culture, or master holds all the keys that will unlock the secret of Self. The mind is inseparable from this Self. As a human being, you are a marvelous composite. Much can be known about you, but the greater part will always remain a mystery. The vibrancy of your being depends on this mystery. Realizing the nature of the Mind and learning to harness its power does not depend on "knowing," as we normally interpret it. There must be a far more subtle connection.

Zen masters often speak of the mind as an ox. An ox is a magnificent, powerful, and wild beast. Like the ox, the mind is also magnificent and powerful, a force of nature that is difficult to control. The idea that is conveyed by the ox metaphor is that your mind must be tamed. If you are not cracking the whip that guides the ox, others are doing it for you or the beast is dragging you here and there as it wills.

If your mind is out of control or under the control of other forces, you are living a diminished life. In fact, you are merely existing. Your every cell should be tinkling with the song of the universe no matter what the circumstances of the day.

We are entering the only type of communion that can help awaken the untouched depths of your mind, a process that can release your spirit from its fleshy prison to dance in the light of divine freedom. Only when we've connected to the truth of ourselves, only when our minds return to Original Nature, can we take our proper stance on Earth.

The world is caught in a violent mind-set. People will kill without hesitation or remorse. A few days before this writing, the news broadcast the story of a man who was so angry that his daughter defied his orders to stay home that when he found the nine-year-old bicycling with a friend, he lost control. He punched the child in the face, then stabbed her to death. This violent act did not satiate his bloodlust. He killed her eight-year-old companion in a similar fashion and hid their bodies in the woods. The case now belongs to the court, but the judiciary cannot get to the root of the problem with punishment. Not even the death penalty will stop the outbreak of similar behavior somewhere else, in someone else. Man has not learned that punishment is only a deterrent to people who are contemplating the consequences of their action. Crimes of passion that explode out of volcanic emotions happen before the conscience can act.

The fragmented mind does not convey true communication. We need to communicate soul to soul, but before this is possible, we must tune into our own souls. To focus the mind is to still it to the point that it becomes a mirror of the Ultimate. When the mind reflects spirit, we are linked to Heaven and Earth. We are whole again.

Realization is not a belief or the result of logic. It results from an unimpeachable connection with the Source. The Source is the incomprehensible origin of all—God, in shorthand. So whether you are driven by science or religious faith, you face the same dilemma. You must give up the prized viewpoint harbored in your mind and cultivate faith in the original nature of Mind. Here is the paradox. If you act from the consciousness of having a mind, you are definitely not okay.

DROP YOUR MIND!

VIII

Munen: Take No-Thought

As humans, we are capable of overcoming incredible challenges. There are some situations that we must approach with our intellect. Problems that exist only within the realm of logic and the laws of the physical universe are unraveled thought by thought. As children, we discovered we could solve a puzzle more effectively by inspecting the full image (goal), then examining the shape and part of that image represented by each piece (the means). We had all the time we needed to solve our recreational puzzles. But life often fires events at us so fast that there is no time to analyze the situation. Perhaps this is what gave birth to the saying "He who hesitates is lost."

Most men imagine that the superior function of the Mind is its ability to think. In the Western Hemisphere, the genius is prized well above the sage. The fruit of the genius is usually accessible to others, even if they fail to grasp the total significance of his discovery. Every schoolchild knows that Albert Einstein discovered the breakthrough formula $E=MC^2$. We all recognized that it represents a great advance in mathematical thinking and opened the doors to practical applications.

Fewer are those who understand the significance or the precision of truth encapsulated in mystical language. Yet the language of the spiritually directed is a science of its own. Used by one who truly "stands under" the influence of direct perception, it penetrates with the depth and accuracy of the most powerful laser. To appreciate such communication, we must approach the subject far differently from the way we approach topics in academia. In schools and universities, the primary tool of discovery is rightfully the thinking mind. The intellect is the tool of knowing. It analyzes the data received by the living computer we call the mind and its related senses. This is not the way of a spiritual seeker. The foundation of our path is Unknowing. To be successful, we must not measure truth by the rod of our intellect. If we embark on our path properly, we will have no tool with which to measure. Measuring mind by mind is dualistic and doomed to failure. How can we achieve One Mind with a divided mind as our tool? Jesus said, "A double-mind is unstable in all of its ways."

That is the diagnosis. What is the treatment? The Bible also says, "Be not conformed to the image of the world but be ye transformed by the renewing of your mind."

If you are the product of a Judeo-Christian upbringing, as is the case with me, it should comfort you to know that neither Jesus nor the Bible refutes the teachings of Buddha and the gurus on the nature of the Mind. In fact, these teachings are supported by the Scriptures, as you will come to realize. This should be no surprise when we remember that God is bigger than our concepts and prejudices allow.

Since we cannot approach the Unknowable with a mind full of what we know (this would be like trying to pour the ocean into a thimble), we must come to it another way. There is no substitute for self-surrender. My own teacher, Sadguru Sant Keshavadas loved to sing "Self surrender is the way," as he played the harmonium. Another way to say this is ego or mind surrender. You can read as many books as you want to, including spiritual literature for inspiration. Any author is happy to have you read his work. God is pleased that you read His words, but are you eating them, drawing the nourishment that will transform you? Are you becoming a new creature? You will never become realized until you drop it. Drop what?

> A monk approached a Zen master carrying a staff.
> "Drop it!" the roshi shouted. The monk let the staff fall to the floor.
> "Drop it!" the roshi shouted again.

> "I have nothing to drop," the bewildered monk replied.
> "Drop it!" the roshi said forcefully.
> The monk was enlightened.
>
> —Paul Reps and Nyogen Senzaki,
> *Zen Flesh, Zen Bones* (Shambhala, 1994)

My martial art is called Zen Mushin Ryu. Like the Aikido of O Sensei Ueshiba Morihei, it is the Way of The Spirit. The name *Zen Mushin Ryu* means that my approach to martial arts arises out of No-Mind. Where there is No-Mind, spirit rules. Zen is synonymous with *munen* (Japanese for "no-thought"). *Mushin* (also Japanese) is another way of saying "no-thought." Jesus Christ admonished his disciples: "Take no thought for what you shall say, and in that self-same hour the Father in heaven will *speak through you*" [italics mine].

No less than the master of Galilee, the Son of God, says in clear speech that if you reach the state of no-thought (munen or mushin), it is the Supreme Himself who orchestrates your speech. Jesus makes it clear that this is how he, Jesus, operates. On the matter of action, he again underscores the vital importance of No-Thought: "The Son can do nothing without the Father."

Jesus is always pointing away from himself: "Not my will but thy will be done." By his example, Jesus demonstrates that his greatness is a by-product of his self-surrender. This surrender of mind to No-Mind, the sacrifice of thought to Munen/No-Thought, is the Universal Way. Something extraordinary happens to a person who lets go of self.

Five hundred years before the birth of Jesus Christ, Siddhartha Gautama, a prince of the Shakya Clan in India, gave up wealth and family name to seek the truth about being. That great sacrifice was not enough. It was not until he surrendered his mind under the Bo tree, giving up his own conscious pursuit of the Way, that he experienced No-Mind and became the person the world now knows today as the Buddha. Shakyamuni, as he is also known, did not create the enlightenment experience. It was already there. By letting go, truth became apparent to him. That same potentiality is in you.

Since I was not born in Asia, people sometimes question how my life could be so closely aligned to "Eastern" spirituality. Where is the abode of No-Mind? There are others who pit their intellectual knowledge against me, flooding my consciousness with facts and figures garnered from many finite sources. All of that is great, if you want to win a debate or write a treatise. The mind is so full of ideas. There are endless ideas and words. No-Mind is empty and serene. There is really nothing to say once you realize it, but as Katagiri Roshi liked to say, we have to say something, so we talk. A robin sings, a snake hisses. These sounds contain just as much truth, just as much Zen, as the utterances of great masters. Do you understand? The real error would be in *trying* to understand me.

I used to run from people who asked me questions or sought me as a teacher. "I have nothing to teach," I said. Those were the good ol' days, the days when I was just emptying myself. Now I do have a sense of mission, and that brings complications and contradictions. How many ways can I say that I teach NOTHING? Empty your own mind of its concepts and expectations and fall, without anything to cling to, into the void and you will discover what I am not saying, what I cannot say.

Where there is no thought of action, where will the explanation of the moves come from? There is a trinity in this practice, *No-Mind, No-Thought, No-Reflection, Mushin, Munen, Muso*. If one is not to reflect, the matter is finished, completely burned out, as Shunryu Suzuki put it in *Zen Mind, Beginner's Mind.*

If I have learned anything in my lifelong quest to unravel the mystery of my existence, it is that there is a difference between religion, the belief and worship of a conceptual and dogmatic God, and Realization. The God of religion, by the very nature of the approach, is definable. The reality is not so. To approach truth from the confinement of an institution is to ferry across the ocean. To realize reality is to be the single drop of water that drops back into the ocean. By this metaphor, Sadguru Keshavadas demonstrated the principle of oneness with God. The drop does not lose its persona, but gains the power and fullness of the Ocean. It is important to note that every drop that allows itself to fall into the ocean will become the ocean without taking away from the consciousness of any other drop. This is Cosmic Mind. This is fulfillment of Zen practice and the ultimate goal of religion.

The journey to a Mind Like Water is a personal one. Yet there is no limit to how many people can experience it. The Bible says, "How can they hear without a preacher?"

One who is preaching the nature of God inspires us to seek. The Bible also poses this question: "How can they learn without a teacher?"

So you believe in the possibility. How do you get there? Zen saying: When the student is ready, the teacher will appear.

The teacher does not come to those who need to be convinced. Let them go to the preacher. The teacher is for those who believe and are ready to take the steps to fulfill the promise. I remember how, in the simple years, I would sit and listen to the sounds of flowing water and the passing ships on the banks of the Elizabeth River in Portsmouth, Virginia. I would just sit and listen.

Without thought, without dependence on what you know, show me your truth right now!

Too late! You were cut three times before you saw one pass of the blade.

Stop thinking! The sword is slicing through the air. If you look at the keen blade glistening, you are dead. The Zen way is to take no thought for what action to take, nor meditate over the danger. Movement is then natural, fluid . . . whoosh! You are gone beyond the danger.

Once again, this understanding is not limited to the Zen of Japan. The biblical King David said in Psalms 144: "Blessed be The Lord my strength who teacheth my fingers to fight and my hands to make war."

David was a "Zen" warrior, also. His skill did not arise from his ego-mind but from the guidance of the Spirit.

In Sanskrit, the word for this instinctive wisdom is *Prajna.* Prajna is one of the virtues, along with *Dhyana* (Zen/Meditation) and *Dana* (Giving). The virtues are not to be viewed as a philosophy. It is more accurate to view them as an observation. The Realized Soul will instinctively meditate, express wisdom, and give openheartedly. At first, the disciples of the Way may emulate those who demonstrate these qualities. When their breakthrough comes, these virtues will be effortlessly expressed.

IX

Recognize the Problem

There is great interest in the spiritual path today, but this interest does not translate into spirituality. As I travel around the globe on Dharma (spiritual) missions, I am made aware of a common problem that persists in the minds of those who boast a Western education. Many people believe that mere knowledge about spiritual traditions and teachers has some type of value beyond being intellectual currency. The simple truth is that knowledge itself will not translate into realization. Knowledge will not reveal the mystery of Self to anyone, and pursuit of the path in this manner is a sure route to deepening the effects of *maya* (illusion). The spiritual path is a paradox. The greatest paradox is that the so-called Path is nonexistent. It is a fabrication of language, albeit for a good reason. Speaking of means, the Bible cites the "ways" of God in this manner, "above the understanding of men." It is clear to me that the word "ways" in this usage means the same as the word *upaya* (skillful means). God uses means to fulfill his plan that cannot be comprehended by man. His methods may make no sense to the ego.

In Asia, the light of realization that passes between master and disciple is revealed as a "tacit understanding." The truth of it, in plain terms, is passed on silently. For any seeker to tap into the secret place within the self, he must place himself in a position to receive. The very existence of a "receiving mind" is an indication that there is a Mind of "transmission."

The truth of being is not bound to any location on the map. East and West as geographic locations are only symbolic, but how we approach the quest is all important when it comes to uncovering the secret of who or what we are in the scheme of the universe. It has long been foreseen that the "Light of Asia" must one day shine brightly in the West, as well:

> Like lightning flashing from the east to the west
> so shall be the coming of the Son of Man.
>
> —Matthew 24:27

That light must shine in the four quarters of the world in order for mankind to return to its primordial roots. For this to happen, the language of awakening must accord with the time and place called "here and now" without losing its original authority.

Through the ages, the term "lineage" is used to recognize disciples of the Way who have received their authority to teach directly from a living master. The only authority is that which has been sealed Mind to mind. It is by this silent "transmission" that the integrity of the Original teachings remains unchanged through the centuries. The personality of each master is different, the cultures may differ, but the fundamental teachings that lead to Awakening are immutable.

Soul to Soul is written to fulfill a vow made to my Dharma predecessor, Sadguru Sant Keshavadas of the Vishwa Shanti Temple in the Himalayas.

It grieved him that the spirituality of the West produced a dogmatic hybrid of the real thing. He saw so much more potential. Perhaps his most poignant point was made when he focused on a particular problem that plagued African Americans. "Black people are very spiritual people," he said. But he stated that black people have no power. "If they learn to harness the power of their minds, black people can have anything they want on Earth. Teach them to harness that power, Kitabu Shyam," he said.

Ironically, while people of diverse cultures are attracted to my mission, the very people I am charged to help hardly know I exist, nor do they know the nature of the work. It is by traveling so much and listening to so many questions that I have come to recognize the misconceptions people have about the nature of the spiritual path, or the Way. *Soul to Soul* is a journey, a kind of show-and-tell book on spiritual ascension. There is a reason why spiritual teachers on the time line from the Buddha to the Christ and modern Zen masters, gurus, and preachers tell stories to illustrate their points. We need clues to escape delusion, but there is nothing that can be said in language that will open the cosmic door. The illustrations of the masters baffle the intellect, but they speak directly to the spirit of man.

Soul to Soul is not a mere esoteric treatise. It underscores real-life experiences in which the power of the Awakened Mind and all it entails kicks in and reveals new dimensions to what first appears to be routine. This includes dark episodes. There is no light without shadows.

Human beings are far more than what science can explain. We are deeper than what is implied in our worship services. Words, even words spoken from a pulpit, do not take the listener into the place of transformation. It takes more. No one can be shoved through the gate of transformation and renewal. No one can be forced to wake up, but, more important, believing in the power to wake up is not an indication that you will; more is required of you.

If you would travel soul to soul you must strip bare. Nothing of this world can pass through the gate. You can pick up what you left behind on your return, if you *want* to return. Some books promise to give you power to control your destiny. If mankind knew what to do with such power, the world would not be so chaotic and unbalanced. If your computer went awry, you would opt to return it to the original factory configurations. People fear to do that with their minds, and so they function with active "viruses" sabotaging their perceptions.

There are millions of people who dream of a heaven to which they will go after death. To the Realized Soul, Earth and Heaven are branches of the same tree. Do you want to help the world? Tame your own mind first. Something extraordinary will happen. When you understand the secret, you can drink a cup of coffee at a café and have an effect on Congress between the first sip and the last.

"What is the sound of one hand clapping?"

While reading *Soul to Soul,* meditate on the empty spaces between each word. Get ready for the answer that will free you from the power of "the Matrix," forever.

X

Entrapment by Conformity

In the Western Hemisphere, to be educated is to undergo a mapping of the intellect so that the student conforms to a proscribed system of learning that will leave him knowledgeable in certain areas. He learns an official history of his locality and country when he is very young. The power of the written words underscored by the voice of a teacher he has been taught to trust gives the images and cultural cues the power of religious dogma, as the young minds generally absorb the teachings without resistance. Students are taught mathematics. They learn that the world conforms to fixed laws. One plus one is two. The unknown quantity *X* can be found, if they just do the math as taught. There is geography. The world is divided and locked into meridians, latitude, and longitude. There is a name for every place, a name for every tribe of man.

And so the young mind probes science. There is an explanation for everything, we believe, even if we do not yet know what it is. The students of our world are taught to search for answers, but the answers are already sealed and coded. A right answer brings a reward; a wrong answer signifies failure. Graduate from school, learn to speak as those before you have done, and doors may open. There is more money to be made, more "toys" to be purchased. Pavlov's dogs were conditioned to salivate at the ringing of a bell. They stood a better chance of being true to their Original Nature than does modern man.

A trap was sprung for your spirit. It is not made of brick or steel, but its strength to bind is immeasurable because of its subtlety. Like a dolphin caught in a tuna net it could not see to avoid, you are caught in an invisible net that is drowning you. The saddest thing about your dilemma is that you probably think you are okay. The worst kind of trap lures you in. It is attractive, sometimes hypnotic, like the intoxicating song of the sirens who lured sailors to cast their ships on the rocks or swim out to be drawn beneath the waves of the ocean.

When I was a boy of about ten, my father talked to me about my growing up. "When you get to 18, you will be a man. You'll have to move out. You have to go out into the world on your own and make your own life," he said. When he said that, I saw myself standing at the door as he stood there holding it open. I looked past him, but I saw nothing out there, not a single thing.

The world outside was a pure etheric white, void of any distinction whatsoever. The vision frightened me because it appeared that I had no future. What I understand now is that I had no concept of the world. My mind was not showing me "nothing," per se; it was the screen onto which not a thing had yet been projected. The scene was a dynamic one filled with infinite possibilities. I did not see a field of nothing. Nothing is negative. I saw before me "vast emptiness," the field of No-Mind. The possibilities ahead were infinite. I just did not understand it then.

XI

Tathagatha

This world can be measured by time, space, and dimensions of height, width, depth, color, sound, and other data perceivable by our senses. It is because it can be touched, seen, heard, and smelled that it can be described in terms of the senses inherent in our bodies. The world itself is an extension of our senses, which is why the way in which we view it can be manipulated by how those senses are triggered and teased. What we generally refer to as the five senses would have no value without the great medium that adds depth, flavor, meaning, and cohesion to what they convey. That medium is the mind.

It is customary for people in the West to consider the brain the intelligence behind our being. Perhaps this is because when a person attaches to what is seen as the real, they apply the same criteria to themselves. From my perspective, the brain is only the hardware. It is but the housing for the wiring and sensors that operate the bio-ambulatory vehicle driven by the real intelligence, which is formless. There is a fundamental error that escapes us in the education process. We are educated from a point of presumed ignorance toward a goal of presumed intelligence. While this programming is designed to guide us into thinking and acting in a certain manner, it fails to explore or unveil the vital truth. *What is Man?* This is not an academic question. Not understanding the uniqueness of his being, the unwitting child is placed into a "machine" designed to destroy or radically alter his fundamental nature. Without help, he will grow up with only a faint glimmer, a speck of light, hinting at his awesome inheritance.

Since our viewpoint about life and the world is being guided at an early age, it is unwise to assume that any definition given us about ourselves is accurate. Even if our beloved teachers of this world wanted to tell us the truth about ourselves, they would have to know the answer themselves. The powers of the world, government, industry, the movers and shakers who prey on the ignorance of ordinary people benefit from your lack of understanding about your own true nature. To penetrate the darkness of ignorance and uncover the power inherent in your breath-energy would cause what Darth Vader of the movie *Star Wars* refers to as "a disturbance in the Force." When a single person breaks free of the net, the ripples create a tidal-wave effect. Sooner or later, every living being connected to the ocean of life will feel the surge. For some of us, this will be a good thing. It will energize our souls like an infusion of the Holy Spirit during a church revival, but for others, the conscious enemies who feed off the weakened spirits of humankind, it will be frightening, a debilitating drain on their resources.

For certain, there are those of you who sense you are caught in a trap. Yet, even with the power of that intuition to guide you, it alone cannot provide the insight strong enough to break you free of the trap. The way out cannot be seen.

Our Original Nature, the True Home, is not accessible from the state of mind our education has produced. The tools used to teach the things of this world have no application to that which predates the forming of the world itself. There is nothing for the teacher to teach but the fact that we are deceived, and to share the words of poets, philosophers, prophets, sages, and seers. In the churches and temples around the globe, the element of faith is introduced. Our source is the Scriptures. If we accept them as divine messages, we have hope. If we do not, we flounder in a sea called despair.

The quoting of the gifted ones provides solace, but liberation cannot be found by quoting or memorizing their words. Liberation cannot be experienced through such means. Scriptures are medicine but not a cure for what truly ails us. Is it enough to sit in a prison and talk of freedom with those who have never soared beyond the dark gray walls? Is there an answer to be found from those who can only imagine what freedom is? If we are crying out for a way, is there anyone who hears those cries?

It is quoted in the Book of Jeremiah, in the Old Testament of the Bible, "If you seek me with all your heart, you will surely find me." As stated earlier, when it comes to the Scriptures, you can choose to believe them or not. I made my decision in my childhood and have never deviated from it. Holy books are the gospel to me. If you are going to use a map as a guide to an unknown destination, you must trust the giver of the map or there is no point in taking off on the journey. If you begin at some point to discount the truth of the document, your enthusiasm will start to wane and your mind will become dualistic. You must choose to go forward anyway, though beset by doubt. Liberation requires great faith. Faith is spiritual fuel. To stop and turn around is the loss of faith. There is no spiritual progress without faith.

The linear world, the world of hustle and bustle, good and evil, stress and distress, reward and punishment, is maintained because our minds are shaped by circumstances that we are lead to believe are the basic criteria of our existence. We are taught how to interpret the data received by our senses in such a way as to produce either conformity or an expectation of conformity. The resulting effect is precisely the opposite of the result promised by the Lord. The world considers those who conform to be good citizens. Yet we are taught by the Scriptures, "Be not conformed to the image of the world but be ye transformed by the renewing of your mind." The message is a spiritual formula. *Do not conform to the image of the world. Be transformed/be changed by the renewing/restoring of your mind.* In our high-tech world, we could say that our minds need to be restored to the original factory configurations.

Meditate on that for a moment. Do you have any idea what your mind would be at this moment if it were suddenly zapped back to the original "factory" specs? If your answer is "Yes, I do have an idea," you are as far from the truth as possible for a person still breathing. Most people, even those who say they are meditating, are not really doing so. It is a subject we shall explore in greater detail in another chapter. The truth is beyond ideation. If you have an idea, that idea stands as a huge mountain blocking your path.

In answer to an earlier question yes, there is ONE who hears our cries, the ONE who does not fall within the matrix cast by the mind of men. The ONE is the original, as in the "original factory configuration." In the West, there is great pride in the accomplishments of the mind. There is pride in being in control. Although these achievements may be lauded by other men, they have no spiritual value and do not move us a single step toward the freedom of mental liberation or enlightenment. In cultures where "egos" are celebrated, it is difficult to yield. Yielding is a necessary act if you want to unlock the secret that will restore your mind to its original nature. A great prize waits, which cannot be reached by grasping.

We enter the world in a state of *sunyata* (emptiness). We take things as they reveal themselves to us without meditation. Later, we cease to trust our initial pure perception and learn about the world from others. From the standpoint of my Christian upbringing, I recognized the Bible as a source of great spiritual teachings. Both my parents expressed their trust in the veracity of the document without equivocation. Every night before my siblings and I went to bed, we were read to from the Book and quizzed. The Bible was indelibly imprinted on our consciousness. There was also the Christian community of our church.

Though I have heard many people outside the Christian experience criticize Christians, something I fully understand, I know from my own 47 years of conscious experience that the Christ experience is profound, deep, purveying peace and love to the willing recipient. Since I came to that personal realization as a boy, I embraced the Spirit of the teachings, escaping the dogmatic and institutional snare that usually awaits followers. In other words, I found for myself the Living Lord of which the Scriptures spoke, the Light emanating from the form, the Light in the darkness. Thus began a lifelong Guru-chela (Master-disciple) relationship. I was nine. Everything was possible then—everything.

We only have words for that which falls within the realm of conceivability. A thing does not have to exist to warrant a word; it just has to be at least a figment of the mind. Where words can attach, forms and concepts take shape. By the use of words, we can convey even the imagined to others. By this means, we bring fictional characters to life. They can possess such vivid lives and their stories can be told so often that they may seem to be breathing beings.

No matter what our ancestral background may be, if we were born in America, the dominant mind, the guiding mind has a Western bent. The most prominent settlers were white men from Europe. The British crown once ruled the Colonies and the majority of the inhabitants came from British soil, British streets, British prisons. Those men and women did not come to a new land to learn a new way of life. What we see by the record they left is that they came to a new country and sought to impose their will on it and the existing inhabitants.

Almost from the beginning, the view of "The Others" (the rulers of the world from my book *The Secret of Freedom*) was clear: There is but one way; our way is the law. By this simple agreement, everyone else is immediately the outlaw. If you were not one of the Others, if you did not fall within that narrow definition of the human being, you fell outside the protection of the law and even beyond the grace of God, so far as human beings were concerned.

As the Others isolated themselves from the original inhabitants of the land morally, legally, and socially, so also did they retreat from the universal core of their being. A kind of spiritual myopia developed. It develops in any culture anywhere that people choose to define what constitutes humanity. Add greed and attachment and there arises the conditions for a holocaust. As one people label another people savages, uncivilized, or unworthy for any reason, they give themselves permission to ignore their own humanity. It is at that moment that true savagery arises, as the self-deemed superior people feel justified in annihilating the "unworthy." What we can learn from the attitude of racism is that those who possess that flaw have a need to feel superior, and it does not matter who or what those they choose to feel superior to may be. First, the Native American is considered inferior, then the African is called inferior, later the Chinese are recognized as inferior. Where there is no other division available, there is a need to paint different nationalities as inferior. When that mind is in charge of the education of the nation, the bias is there even when it is no longer consciously intended.

If the world is viewed only through blue-tinted glasses, golden grains of wheat and expansive fields of corn will never be ripe for harvesting. An unaffected observer could advise the farmer to take off his glasses and the problem will be solved. Who is there to help when the problem is deeper? Who can direct us when the problem is the National Mind?

Scientists deal with what they can see and prove. Some scientists believe that when a habit is established in a species over a period of time, it becomes genetic. It is passed on through the genes to others who have had no direct contact with those originally affected. In what is called the hundredth monkey phenomenon, researchers observed that some monkeys in an island monkey colony, before eating the sweet potatoes the researchers left on the beach for them, washed them first to remove the sand. Before long, all the other monkeys in the colony began doing the same thing. That chain of events was quite astounding, but it was even more startling when it was discovered by another team of researchers that monkeys on another island, who had no contact with the first colony, began washing their food also. The suggestion of a type of cellular communication between beings in the same species may be new to scientists, but it is nothing special to those who experience Original Nature through direct experience.

The very definition of Zen is a direct pointing at the soul of man, a tacit understanding outside of the Scriptures (written word), not dependent on words (spoken) or letters . . .

It is because we depend so much on words and letters, what is spoken and written, that we do not remember how to learn or know without them. This dependency leaves us as vulnerable to manipulation as our computers are vulnerable to viruses. The mind that believes in its superiority and the mind that believes in its inferiority are equally afflicted with disease. But there is a cure. You cannot find the cure, however. It is enough to accept that you possess the mind virus.

There is a part of you yearning to break free, the experience of which will make your greatest day seem like a nightmare. It is true that "the Matrix has you," as *The Matrix* movie trilogy suggests, but how it has you is another story. No movie can cover the breadth and width of the truth. The apostle Paul said, "We see through a glass darkly." What you don't see is immeasurable. What you don't see, what you cannot see with the mind, is the answer. Does that mean there is no hope for freedom?

The Bible states, "You shall know the truth and the truth shall set you free." You may think you know the truth already, so I pose a simple test question. Are you free? If you are, can you manifest that freedom in your daily life? In my travels, I have come to see that people believe the truth to be a series of ideas they can convey in sentences. The Word, to them, is the written marks on paper with chapter and verses clearly visible. It is clear that they do not understand the ancient and original meaning of such terms as "the Word." It is because they have adapted to the use of the wrong faculty for spiritual understanding that they fall far short of their potential.

Christ is called the Great Physician. Christians know him as the great healer of the soul. The office of the spiritual physician has more than a single practitioner. Whereas the spirit of the Physician is one, the vessels that act as channels for its power are many. Although those who appear on Earth in the name of the Lord serve different functions or have specific missions, they are under the authority of the Supreme Power (or they act counter to the well-being of humankind). It is a lineage that goes back to the beginning of time when such emissaries of the Divine may have been called prophets or sages.

The term *guru* means dispeller of darkness. It is used to connote men and women who have a direct and conscious link to Original or Universal Mind. It is the uniqueness of this Unborn Mind that gives the guru the power to see things as they really are, not as they appear to be. It is that nature within the guru that allows him to act as a living guide to those who would be navigated past the traps that bind the mind and imprison the soul. For the true guru, the path emerges with every step. He knows nothing, in the sense that what he has learned while in the world is not the source of his wisdom. His understanding and actions rise from no-thought (munen) and no-reflection (muso). They are pure and spontaneous flashes from emptiness.

The physical presence of a guru or Tathagatha is subject to the laws of cause and effect in this world; if he is caught speeding, he can expect a ticket. His actions, however, produce no karma. In other words, a Tathagatha or guru is perfect spiritually because the experience transcends the realm of good and evil. This might seem a huge stretch for any religious-minded person to believe, especially Christians, until you view it against the teachings of the Scriptures about the true nature of Man. Jesus said, "Be ye perfect as I am perfect." So how can a person, any person, dot every *i* and cross every *t?* Jesus said it this way, "The Son can do nothing without the Father." The mind of the guru is No-Mind. No-Mind is Tathagatha. Tathagathas emanate from beyond mind. As best as can be translated into terms that are familiar in Judeo-Christianity, anyone sent in the role of a Tathagatha or guru has a mind in the likeness of Melchizedek or Christ, unified with THAT (identified only as Father) by Jesus.

The word *Tathagatha* translates as "thus come and thus go." It is a suggestion of appearing and disappearing without a trace. The Old Testament speaks of Melchizedek as a priest forever, a man without mother or father, no beginning or end of days. Jesus is said to be after the order of Melchizedek. This is a major revelation. To be *after the order of* clearly reveals that there exists a spiritual lineage. There is the lineage of the eternal priesthood, of which Jesus is an extension, not the beginning. By the very nature of orders and lineages, there are others.

What we know of the order of Melchizedek is all we need to understand. Melchizedek was directly linked to the Supreme or Father Spirit, as would be Jesus after him. He was a single individual. He experienced himself according to his spiritual not carnal nature, thus he was without attachment to time, not subject to dissolution. If one is after the order of Melchizedek, he or she is of the Unborn. The essence of his or her life draws from the eternal not the ephemeral. Those of this priesthood connect to mankind in a different way from the priests who serve in temples, churches, or the like. These priests are undivided. They stand on the authority of the I Am; there is no division between them and the One.

The work of such priests as this, by whatever title they may be known, does not conflict with the work of anyone who is of the same lineage. It is like standing before a mirror. The image seen and the image observing are powered by one mind and spirit. However one moves or dances, the reflection is in accord. The Tathagatha acts without hesitation because there is no second mind in him, no other way to make him waiver. Thus Jesus could say with full authority, "I am the way, the truth and the life." Krishna said with equal authority, "I am the me in everyone."

Speaking of Tao (the Way), Lao Tzu said, without apology, "I do not know its name, but it is the Mother of all things."

Those who experience the indefinable for themselves do not waiver when speaking, writing, or acting on that understanding. There is just clarity, clean clear through. If this was not so, who would have faith to follow a master one step into the Unknown? Who would dare risk their soul when the teacher doubts?

The appearance of Adam was a brilliant flash of instant consciousness. Adam was a Tathagatha. Everything he needed to live fully and completely was contained in that single instance of recognition of his environment. He needed nothing more. He ceased to function as Tathagatha the moment he hesitated and accepted a SECOND mind as an authority over his. "A double-mind is unstable in all of its ways," Jesus said. The moment the immediacy was gone, a lesser man or mental being came into awareness.

A Tathagatha is not dualistic. The dualistic Adam was not the Tathagatha Adam. The Tathagatha still illuminated the higher realm of consciousness, but Adam could no longer access the way. "*The Light shines in the darkness but the darkness comprehends it not.*"

The story of Adam is like the hundredth monkey story. We can rename it the E Pluribus Unum story, "out of one comes many." Adam doubted the unimpeachable authority of his own being and relied on a second opinion, and in some way or another, you have been relying on the "authorities" of the Others ever since. "Monkey see, monkey do," we used to play as children. The gurus call the ego-mind, Monkey Mind; who is your mind imitating and why? There is no imitation of the real thing. You have to be the real thing. Monkey Mind is playing tricks and your spirit remains a prisoner in a prison cell where the bars are disguised as the truth.

To say "the world that mankind has created" is the same thing as saying "the world that mind has created." In Sanskrit, the word "man" is *manu* or "mental being." What you see as the world is the mind superimposed on matter. Sadguru Sant Keshavadas taught that if the mind plays tricks, it is not harmful for it to superimpose the image of a snake upon a rope lying in the grass. You may be frightened, but it will do you no harm. On the other hand, there is a serious problem if your mind superimposes the image of a rope on a snake. If you pick up the rope/snake, you put yourself in jeopardy. That story is a hint of a how a spiritual teacher/physician works. Stories, poems, music, anything may be used as "medicine" to treat the condition of the mind. These tools do not appeal to logic, but stoke the intuition through *upaya* or skillful means. Thus a guru, roshi, or any such teacher need not use any fixed pattern or method to help you. He must simply apply the tool that will catapult you into empty space. Only there can you meet your true self, shorn of all trappings.

To embark on this journey, you must do the opposite of what you would normally do when preparing to embark on a quest of some sort. You have bags. Unpack those bags! There is a Zen saying: "From the first not a thing is." The statement mirrors the biblical verse in Genesis: "In the beginning God created the heavens and the earth." Since God is not a thing and has no beginning by definition, both teachings point to the womb of Zen, which is No Mind, No Thing. Once having lost even the memory of our Original Mind, where do we go for help?

Only the "factory-authorized" dealer can service your CPU, your central processing unit, your mind.

Spiritual teachers, by any name you choose to call them, are authorized to restore your mind. They are fully licensed for the job and can use any tools or means necessary to complete their task. They come directly from "headquarters" and recognize no other authority. It is a simple formula. There is the Supreme who is untraceable by the finite; there is the manifested form hotwired to Universal Mind. While each form possesses a unique personality and perspective, that form is empty. The Universal Mind is the same Universal Mind at work in each chosen vessel. It is as if you installed pipes in a housing unit. Although each resident would have their own faucet, they would be drawing water from the same source. The Universal Mind is Guru, the Universal Mind is Roshi. Anyone tapping into that mind, whether chosen at birth or through enlightenment after birth, speaks as one with all the masters who came before. This is the lineage spoken of earlier, as in the order of Melchizedek: "Let this mind which was also in Christ Jesus, be also in you."

While this is so, each guru or roshi, each spiritual teacher has a little something that ties him or her to the world of mankind, something that causes him or her to remain sympathetic to the contradiction of being human embracing the divine. What could it be?

> An ox jumped through a window. His massive head and magnificent horns, his hooves and his entire body all passed through but his tail could not.
>
> —Zen koan

Viewed logically, it makes no sense that an ox could pass through a small opening and his tail alone would fail to cross over. That is why parables and Zen koans exist. They are means to develop the powers of perception beyond the realm of logic. Jesus spoke in parables, and he did so to defy the conceptual mind of the day. He spoke parables not to be understood by his listeners intellectually, but to trigger the movement of their spirit.

A guru or roshi may lament for a long time over the contradictions in his own being. One day, he realizes that it is not his own being that he is lamenting over. By the nature of his office, he is in a state of *muga* (Japanese for no-self). He is experiencing the brokenness of man through his body. It is because he can feel the suffering and conflicts of man as his own that he is in position to be of service to humanity. The data received from his unit/being is processed by Universal Mind, which, in turn, works out a solution that will eventually seep into the consciousness of man as a whole. "If I be lifted up from the earth, I will drawn all men unto me," Jesus said.

Those who are sent from the "Home Office" for spiritual missions do not speak for themselves. They have a will. "Not my will but thy will be done," Jesus said. They surrender their will. When that happens they are no longer personal beings, belonging to some finite category, they are impersonal. They speak with the authority of the Great I AM, by speaking *as* the Great I AM. They do not split themselves in two but speak in oneness. So Jesus said, "I and the Father are One," but he also qualified that statement with, "I would ye be one as we are one." This established that the same relationship was possible for you to have.

As noted previously, the word "religion" comes from the root word *religare,* which means "to bind." The inward path is taken to break the yoke, to destroy bondage of every kind. It is the route taken only by those who believe it is their birthright to be utterly free. After all, if one is in the likeness of his parent and that parent is God, what binds God? What is God afraid of? Sooner or later, your journey to freedom will bring you up against iron barriers, difficult to pass. The challenge you face will be your conventional way of thinking.

Without coming in contact with the teachings of Jesus Christ, Siddhartha Gautama, known for thousands of years as the Buddha, or the Awakened One, became enlightened to that mind and spoke with authority himself.

If you think about it, you would probably say what a misguided fellow. If you are a Christian, you might get angry and think he claimed a spot only Jesus can claim, but then again, you would be using logic. You would be thinking there could be only one, and therefore someone has to be false.

That is why the Home Office sends Tathagathas into the world. "To some he sent preachers. To others he sent teachers." How can they hear without a preacher? How can they learn without a teacher? How many times do you have to read or hear this before you realize that the preacher and the teacher spoken of in this verse are not the same. We live in a world where the authority and presence of God are now largely ignored. I often hear people say, "He is both a preacher and a teacher." The preacher/teacher educates and illuminates the Scriptures but the master/teacher illuminates the mind. His mission is to direct the prodigal back to the Father now, not at some future time. The preacher/teacher speaks to the congregation, the flock. The master/teacher speaks only to the disciple. The master/teacher walks and lives in the reality of the power. He can demonstrate his connection to the Father in real time, whenever the need arises.

In the religious community, the preacher has become the most recognized "spiritual" worker, and as such has nearly blotted out the office of other agents of God from the mind of the believer. Thus the spiritual teacher is hardly spoken about. He is not alluded to from the pulpit, or is seen by most people as another function of their pastor, perhaps an office under the institutional church. It has been forgotten that those who performed such roles in the past acted outside of the "church leadership" and abided in the "secret place" of the Most High. They appear when necessary and depart when their missions are over. A Tathagatha is like empty air. His words and deeds are lightning bolts illuminating the night sky.

The empty air does not cling to the lightning bolt, neither does it know when or how it will strike. It is simply the medium through which the power passes. Inwardly, the Tathagatha is empty. He is alive but not attached to a fixed identity.

Sadguru Sant Keshavadas, speaking to devotees in the Temple of Cosmic Religion where he taught Dharma to the people of the West, described the experience as being like a straw. The straw is visible in our drink. We can touch it. Yet the purpose of the straw is not fulfilled in how it looks but in the hollow center. It is empty through and through. Guruji discussed how God is not only able to draw the spirit of mankind (the liquid) through the upper end of the straw, but he is also able to blow his breath through the straw back into mankind.

The straw allows the free-flowing of the spirit of mankind to God and the flowing of God into the earthly regions that mankind inhabits. By means of this body we are calling the straw, mankind and God function as one. They share a single mind: No-Mind. It is just this nature that is called Buddha in Sanskrit. The word *Buddha* does not mean a God. When we no longer conform to the image of the world, when we are transformed by the renewing of the mind, the new creation that emerges is called, in that ancient tongue, Buddha. You could say that Adam is back, as good as new.

Buddha is not a particular person, neither is he a thing or a concept. We cannot discern or apprehend Buddha through our thought processes. Those who are preordained to become spiritual teachers of mankind naturally flow from the spiritual center where life originates to the finite. They do not question the mystery of their being, but wholly accept it. It is in the world where human beings function within the realm of cause and effect, time and space, good and evil, life and death, the world where the mind is fragmented, that the Tathagatha learns the difference between direct perception and conceptual thinking.

A Tathagatha develops his personal style of teaching as he walks in the body and encounters people and experiences events. The Tathagatha sees everything from the stillpoint of the Uncreated interfacing with the created world. While a Tathagatha has no self, per se, a sense of self arises as actions and reactions to phenomenon in this world produce a protocol program that is logged into the computer we call a brain. This guidance system permits the spirit-centered being to function in the world where seeing is believing and matter is the foundation upon which human consciousness rests. The Tathagatha is valuable to God because he can freely move among free-willed humans and interact. He is valuable to mankind because he dwells in Original Nature. Thus he is linked between the world of appearance and that which is beyond phenomenon. He can help because he bridges the gap between this and that. The Tathagatha himself has no philosophy, concepts, or religion, but he can use what is accessible. Guruji uses the analogy of the proverbial swan.

The swan floats upon the water. It has a wonderful ability. It can be given a mixture of water and milk, drink the milk, and leave the water. Guruji was revealing how a guru, who is also of Tathagatha nature, can read the Scriptures and discern the hidden message. A guru or Tathagatha need not be born in a particular religious setting or to a given nationality. Wherever he appears, his ability will manifest in that environment.

"Truth is one. Many are the names," masters teach. Wherever we open our eyes for the first time, our nature is the same, God is the same, truth is the same. Nothing we say or do can alter what is. If we do not discern that we are being deceived, the lie will be the only world we know. The moment we discover something is amiss, help can come. "If you seek me with all your heart, you shall surely find me," God says in Jeremiah. "*You will surely find me.*" If it is God who teaches "seek and ye shall find," we have heard it from the highest authority. Seek!

When the student is ready, the master will appear. This is Dharma, the law of the spirit. Have faith in that and your journey becomes a guided adventure.

In *Superman: The Movie,* Lois Lane is falling from a skyscraper and Superman makes his first appearance in his eye-arresting red and blue suit. He catches her many stories above the street. "Don't worry, miss. I've got you."

"You've got me? Who's got you?" she asks in a shocked tone.

That is a legitimate question to ask any spiritual teacher, guru, or roshi who stands before you with a promise to aid you in a way that seems impossible for a human to fulfill.

With complete authority, I tell those who come to me, "I've got you." So who has me?

Who has any guru, roshi, Tathagatha? For the answer to that, you must turn the page.

NO BODY
NO THING . . .
NADA . . .

The guru can help you because he sees only you. While human beings may be seeking their own salvation, the guru lives only to meet the needs of other beings. The impersonal nature of guru is not that which is born to mother and father. Only the body is generated by human parents. The guru, that is, the guru-consciousness (No-Mind), is without birth or death, without beginning or end; thus another term for a guru is a god-man. Such people act in accord with what is presented to them; they are emissaries who come from nowhere, yet that no-where-ness, though not a place, is dynamically alive and intelligent. It is the source/power behind all things.

Men are creatures of free will and they are able to use that will to block vital experiences. The guru is a master of yielding to the unknown. Thus he is an agent of the unknown. *God works in mysterious ways.*

I learned the language my parents spoke. Language is a tool of communicating. Who has me? In the language of my parents, in the language of my church, God has me. In my experience, the Unknown supports me even though I dive through empty space to help whomever I am sent to. How is that possible? When one is, by nature, unborn, there is no source to question. Questions are introduced by outside sources. The Unborn is one with the source of being. It takes dualism to perceive a separate self other than fully being. When there is no attachment to naming or the named, there is just function and perception. A thirsty man does not argue about what the cool refreshing clear liquid is called as it flows down his parched throat and restores his vitality. Agua is agua. It satisfies. Water satisfies. *L'eau* satisfies, *wasser* satisfies, but not because of the sound we call it by. It satisfies simply because the essence and nature of it is unchanged by the sounds used to point it out. It is a reality apart from name.

Words are tools created to imprint our understandings, feelings, or desires on the minds of others. Words are not the only way to do this, but they have become the most prominent, thus most relied upon means. They are the most traveled road from mind to mind, the means to countless dimensions of perception. Therein lie the glory and the danger of words. We hear it often. *Knowledge is power.* Deception, however, can undermine the mind with ease, if applied early enough in life. To misunderstand, or not know, can be corrected, but deception is intentional. There is a plan of continuity. When the stakes are high enough, there is no limit to the damage the perpetrators will do to hide the truth. "Train a child in the way he should go and when he is older he will not depart from it" (Prov. 22:6). One child is trained to be the master, the other is trained to be a slave. It is the natural order. Or is it?

XII

One Article of Faith

It has been said before, but it must be said over and over: Faith is necessary to get to the unknown destination. You may think that you already have faith, and you probably have a lot of faith in various areas. This journey, one that takes you on a trip from soul to soul, requires advanced faith, however, so it is best for us to explore the subject a little. There is no reason to remember what I write. It is seasoning we are after. I want you to have the flavor. That is sufficient.

Have Faith in Your Mind! That Is,
The Original Spotless Mind of No-Mind.

Without faith in the Mind of No-Mind there is no way to enter the kingdom of the soul, the Kingdom of Heaven.

Seek and ye shall find. When we begin a search, whether it is for something we have misplaced or something we simply desire or miss, we set in motion a drive that moves us. If you are looking for your misplaced glasses, you will not be satisfied when you find a lost sock. You will continue to search. If you are at the park looking for a friend you expect to meet there, no stranger will suffice. Let us suppose you are searching for something that is an unknown. You do not know what you need or what it looks like. You only have a feeling of vacancy in your being. If you leave your familiar environment, strap on your backpack, and take to the road, where will you go? Perhaps someone suggests that you take a cross-country trip. Others say travel the sea. Still others advise you to head east. Yet what will you find that will satisfy when you do not know what you are seeking or whom to ask for help?

The deluded, even the brilliantly deluded, can only give you a panacea. Unless your advisor has, himself, realized what you seek, the best he can offer comes nowhere near what you crave.

If the hunger within you is of a spiritual nature, it will never be satisfied by food that is produced by the mind. The highest function of the ordinary mind is the fruit of the intellect. At peak performance, the mind can only conceptualize, imagine, analyze, or stand apart from the experience. It cannot enter into it because it experiences itself as the observer. Thus the Zen teaching, "The eye cannot see itself; the mind as we know it is the imposter." The True Mind, the Mind of Zen, the Mind of Christ, the Original God Mind, does not look back upon itself. So where is help to be found?

The seeker must have faith that there is help. We do not doubt that the Earth exists. We see that there is harmony and intelligence behind its workings. There are plants, and sunlight and water to nourish them. There are birds, and the wind current on which they ride. There is man with the inherent ability to find everything he needs, as it lies hidden in the earth. He learns to fashion the most marvelous things out of raw substance. Whatever man needs or desires, whether or not it is good for him or his fellow man, he is led by his mind to discover it in the material universe. By nature, the mind searches out the secrets of the universe and finds them one by one with the accuracy of a heat-seeking missile. This mind functions in the realm of substance.

The mind and substance, emptiness and form are not one, yet not two. For ordinary people to not know is a vacuum, so they seek to fill that void with knowledge. Their mind moves from the known to the known, attempting to leap over the void as quickly as possible. If you are seeking for the truth of your being, not knowledge about it, but genuine realization, you must lay your sacrifice at the door. There is help. The help was preordained from the first moment we slipped into delusion. The offending instrument cannot be the medium of healing.

The most important thing you need to accept is the office of the spiritual teacher. While the teacher or master may be known by many names and born in various cultures, he is not bound to that culture, even though he reflects various traits native to his land. A true spiritual teacher does not choose himself, but is ordained to that office before he is born. At some point, he will still need teaching, but the seed of the Master is with him from the beginning. Unlike a preacher who speaks to those who listen so that they may become aware of their souls and the need for God, the spiritual teacher is sent directly to souls/spirits. He, being born of the Spirit, addresses only the spirit of mankind, not the mind. Those he meets on the road must recognize him and his office. It is not his place to convince, cajole, seek, or challenge those lacking in faith. Thus the principle holds true: When the disciple is ready, the master will appear.

You must be ready to take the step. If you need to be convinced that there is such a reality as a spiritual teacher or must present 20 questions to the persons you visit, you are not yet ready. How did you find this teacher? Were you impressed by a slick ad, the fame, did he or she look the part? None of that is enough. If you must test a spiritual teacher, and you must, do not come with a list of questions or be influenced by what others say about him or her. That is not enough for you. If you would test a spiritual teacher, try him by the Spirit, test him on the channel you seek. Pray, meditate, discern his spirit, silently, observe. Send a message through the Creator. If it comes back through the master, he is of the Spirit, indeed. Only then can you accept his teachings. Expect the unexpected. There is no absolute and fixed method to break down your delusions. The master uses *upaya,* skillful means. Anything goes, anything. He is working to free your soul from its prison. He does not need the approval of the very mind that holds it there.

Racial consciousness extends to the quasi-spiritual path. People tend to assume that when it comes to the subject of enlightenment, the spiritual teacher is required to look and sound a certain way. It is most often believed that he is the real thing only if he comes from India, Japan, China, or some other Far Eastern address. Sometimes I discern, as I teach, a reluctance on the part of some listeners to believe that a master clothed in the dark skin of African ancestry has the spiritual authority to help them break the yoke of delusion.

Once a woman said after hearing me speak that she was going to go to India and seek enlightenment. I was holding a flute. I cast it to the floor and stood on top of it. "Come join me on top of the Himalayas," I said. "It will save you more than three thousand dollars." The others in the room laughed, but she did not get my message. Months later, she returned from India, sorely disappointed and depressed.

Zen master Bankei said that he had never met anyone who went to India and found a true master. "It is not because there are no true masters in India," he said. When we seek the Unknown with our projections, we have already said what we will accept as true. We block ourselves from receiving a true master even if we are standing before him, because we attempt to measure him with our mind. This will never be successful. Only the spirit can lead us to a spiritual master. The path is beneath your feet and the Master is always before you. When you seek Him in spirit, then He will come to you. You cannot successfully choose the vessel in which He will appear. You will either recognize him by his spirit or you will let him pass by. Your ego has no control on this path.

The last time I saw my grandmother alive was an extraordinarily beautiful experience. On that day, I arrived at a restaurant to have dinner with a friend who was also a disciple of Sadguru Sant Keshavadas. Bharati met me at the entrance to the establishment. When I saw her, a strange vibration penetrated my consciousness.

"Can we postpone this for a few hours?" I asked. "I must go see my grandmother right now this minute."

"Certainly," she responded graciously.

My grandmother was with my aunt Barbara Jean and her husband, George, recuperating from surgery. There had been no indication that she was in any imminent danger. Yet the urging to see her was too powerful. I would not let it pass. When I got to my aunt's house, I spoke to everyone and went into my grandmother's room. I greeted her with a kiss. She was lively, smiling broadly when I entered the room. She lay in a hospital bed that had been brought to the house to make her more comfortable. The two of us chatted as we always did and watched a movie on television.

Then my grandmother revealed a secret to me. "Whenever I am in trouble and need assistance," she said, "I dial the operator. I dial J-E-S-U-S. He is the swiftest operator there is."

I immediately related to that statement because when I experienced satori, one phenomenon I remembered after the fact was that I somehow functioned through the medium of a living connection I nicknamed the swiftest operator in the universe or Zero, for short. My grandmother, whose name was Louise Turner, but renowned as "Miss," a popular midwife, shared this spiritual experience with me. We had always been so close that I could feel her spiritually. She was one of my earliest positive memories. I remember her coming to see me when I was about three. I stood on the bed in my "footed" pajamas while she gave me the greatest hug, which permeated my soul with love vibrations. She had me then, forever.

The "operator" connected us, and I was there with her, enjoying the moment . . . relaxing in love.

"Baby, would you come over and rock the bed for me," my grandmother asked.

The bed had rails. I got up and stood looking down at her smiling face and started to rock the bed gently from side to side. Soon she closed her eyes and drifted into quietness. When I saw that she was asleep, I leaned forward and kissed her on her brow. Then I waved to my aunt and left. It was an excellent visit. I had no immediate understanding about what had happened. My grandmother used to rock me to sleep. This time, I rocked her to sleep and she closed her eyes. It was the final living chapter in our story. The sweet kiss good-bye. Later that night, my aunt called to tell me she was gone. I felt good. Had I ignored the call, I would have been devastated by the loss, but I wasn't.

I was grateful that I had been permitted to meet her in mid-transition so that our parting left a sweet taste in my spirit. If you seek the connection, you will get connected. When the call comes, will you respond faithfully or will you analyze and make excuses as to why you should ignore it? You must be ready. For the warrior, the moment of danger is now. For the disciple of the Way, the moment of obedience is now.

Since there has been much confusion in the world about the matter of what we really are, the nature of God and religion, and the broad subject of spirituality, it is helpful to point out certain misconceptions, as well as to provide support for the veracity of the office of spiritual masters and teachers. Scientific theory is measured against the laws of science. The legal system is guided by written laws. If you want to examine the function of the wind, look at the floating leaf and the bending tree. To appreciate how the spirit operates, you must examine the movement of the spirit in the universal records. Every culture in the world seeks connection with the Unknown, the Source of Life. In every culture, there is a record that a person represented the Unknown, acting as the voice and ambassador for the tribe or nation.

Without discussing religion, specifically, all those who embrace the reality know that God is spirit. It is understood that God as spirit can and does operate through flesh and blood. The body is a medium, a vessel. The toggle switch between the soul of man and the Spirit of God is the mind. Point the mind toward God, the infinite, by the act of surrender or immersion in Him, and one is inseparable from Him. Point the mind toward the flesh and one is carnal. When the mind takes residence in the soul and lives through it, he is once again the son of Man, inheritor of God, he is the willing servant of the Lord, the teacher, the prophet, the preacher. When he rests in the soul, he is lord of himself, Original Man . . . he is home in the garden again. The spiritual teacher is the guide who leads man from the destitute world back to the Garden of Eden. This is only possible while he is alive. Heaven can only be reached through death. Spirits don't die, they just slip into something more comfortable. By definition, man is a living soul or being. Your skin, muscles, flesh, and internal organs are not alive. If you feel that they are, you are functioning within the dimension of the great lie . . . and that is why you need the teacher.

> Like the wind that bloweth where it listeth and thou heareth the sound thereof yet knoweth not from whence it cometh or whither it goeth, so are they that are born of the Spirit. (John 3:8)

As Jesus indicated, those who are born of the spirit are in the world but not of it. As such, they are not trapped by the illusions. In the unfolding of their earth experience, they, too, are engulfed by darkness, but the light within keeps shining through. Darkness cannot snuff it out.

It is by the direct experience of living his own life that the future spiritual teacher learns the power of Spirit. His testimony is true because his experience is personal. The Scriptures are not his source of faith; they simply amplify and confirm what he knows by virtue of his own living connection. They point to the universality of what he, himself, knows in his secret place. The spiritual teacher is intimately linked with the Unknown. Whereas he is the inhalation, God is the exhaler. It is from this vantage point that the spiritual teacher sees into the world. Living by spirit, he recognizes the fundamental nature of all beings, even when they fail to see it in themselves.

Naturally, as natural as a cat climbing a tree or purring contentedly, the spiritual teacher moves and acts in accord with inner nature. By so doing, he sends ripples through the spiritual dimension, the realm of soul. Friends, seekers, foes are all attracted. He responds as appropriate, but the nature of his response does not correspond to a given script. If you want to undercover your hidden nature, do not seek information from a scholar, or guidance from a set system of any kind. They will not take you very far. Seek the spirit by the spirit. He alone will point you to one who stands alone in Him: the roshi, the guru, the "fool on the hill." So God is everywhere? Apparently, that bit of information about the nature of God has not helped the many who search high and low to find him. Admittedly, the Light within is next to impossible to find, so there is the Light of the World. The Light of the World does not shine hidden; it is high, radiating from a living lamp. The Light shining in the world is not the sun. *The Word, the Holy Spirit, is the voice and intelligence of all genuine spiritual teachers. He is the Light shining in the darkness. The spiritual teacher, he of No-Mind, that is, the mind surrendered, is the Lamp.*

If you are sleepwalking, only one who is awake and moving through the same street can lead you home. A person who is dreaming about a sleepwalking person can help neither himself nor the person being dreamed about. No one born of this world is qualified to be a spiritual teacher. He may read all the books ever written and memorize every text, but he is not qualified to address the condition that binds men to the lie. There is no help to be found from anyone whose tool of operation is the mind.

Only that which is born of the spirit can access the spirit. If you cannot grasp that the office of spiritual teacher comes from the Source that created the world, you will not give a master the respect due. If you fail to receive the ambassador, you insult the emperor. You close the gate on yourself. There is no place for ego. Leave your ego at the door with your shoes.

> Man should not live by bread alone but by every word which proceedeth out of the mouth of God. (Matt. 4:4)

Now, if God had said every word that was written in the Book, the subject would be completely covered, with nothing left unsaid. He said, by every word that proceeds from His mouth. A mouth speaks. It does not write. We hear what is uttered. So where is God's mouth, and what is He saying now?

> Take no thought for what you should say and in that same hour the Father will speak through you. (Matt. 10:20)

If you are always talking and thinking, God is silent. The spiritual teacher, however, dwells in the silence, quelling his thoughts. Do not ask him a question if you are not ready to hear the voice of the one who knows. The spiritual teacher has nothing to say.

There is something you must understand when you enter the study of self. Your opinion is worthless. Your knowledge has even less value. The path of realization is not a democratic one. The teacher is the master, period. Once you place yourself under his authority, God and the master are one. It is like sipping a cool drink through a straw. The straw is the means by which you receive the drink. God gives you manageable doses of His being by radiating Himself through the focal point of the master. He personifies as the master. The master is, at the same time, a human being and the infinite presence. Just as the shape of water does not alter its nature, a guru is no less human for his divine core, as God is no less God for merging with the spirit of man in the body of manifestation. Such is the great mystery and marvelous nature of being.

If you are sincere in your quest to uncover the great treasure that is really you, you must recognize that you have set your sights on a course that takes you out of the world of the intellect to a region beyond the most awesome place in the universe.

There is someone who moves in harmony with you when you make that decision and comes toward you from the unknown to an eventual meeting place in the middle ground. So if you are sincere, now is the time to divest yourself of that which hinders your awakening.

Relax. This is a journey of love orchestrated by the Creator of the Universe. Our free will took us way off course, and gently must we be led back. Those who come in His Name love you, too. They are linked across time by other brothers and sisters joined in the soul of humanity. If one falls, all fall, as we learned in the "Garden of Eden." So step-by-step, souls ascend and descend to help us in the great healing. They connect the only way that works, soul to soul. If you have gotten this far, you have most likely felt the stirring in your own spirit. Reach out to the helping hand. One day your hand will throw out the lifeline to others, and so it goes.

> No matter how innumerable sentient beings are, I vow to save them all.
>
> —Zen vow

> Go ye therefore into the world, teaching and preaching whatsoever I have commanded you . . .
>
> —Great Commission of Christ

If one brother falls, there is another brother standing by to catch him . . . this is the Way of the Spirit.

Meditate on that. If you feel the truth of it, then you are ready for one more step.

Royalty is inherited. It is a lineage that continues from generation to generation. The Word, the active power of God, passes from soul to soul. The Mind, the Original Mind, Buddha, if you will, is also ever-present, revealing itself through those who become awake. The Awakened Ones personify this Mind, as Christ personified the Holy Spirit. The Awakened Ones are the Mind made flesh. Spirit and Mind are not the same. The Scriptures warn us that there is a natural conflict between the two. If that is so, then what?

The Scriptures also tell us that God created two great lights, the sun to rule by day and the moon by night. The problem is solved. As long as the sun is contented to shine in the day and the moon at night, their kingdoms are clear. For the sake of clarity, let us agree that the Mind is the moon and the Sun is the Spirit. The mind functions in the realm of creation. It is made useful by the presence of the material universe and the body, which is an aspect of that universe. The Mind, holistically speaking, is emptiness (without form) and form. Aware of form and function, it is the mind. It is dualistic in nature. Nonattached to form or substance, not grasping or even clinging to the notion of its own existence, it is No-Mind. No-Mind is the same thing as Buddha, as Buddha is meant to suggest. A person experiencing life as such is a member of the Royal House. He is a Number One Son, or she is a Number One Daughter. Their kingdom is not in question.

When viewed against the teachings of the enlightened ones, we learn and can experience for ourselves that enlightenment awakens a soul in the Buddha Realm. If you substitute the words "Kingdom of Heaven" for "Buddha Realm" and remember that Christ taught that the kingdom was within and among us, you may be able to discern that, unlike heaven, a place set aside for the many, this kingdom resides solely within the realm of your own being. It is taught that Mind is Buddha. The Heaven of a Buddha is the endless field of his own Original Mind expressing itself as he himself.

Christianity and Judaism teach that man is created in the likeness of God. Belief is not the ultimate experience. It is the prerequisite for steps of faith. It should be encouraging to believers that a term such as "Buddha" exists in the world. It underscores and reinforces the original design of Man. The Bible tells us that the original man had dominion over all the Earth and all within it. He was Lord of the Earth. This is Mind over matter. It is also clear, that, originally, man acted from tacit understanding, not thought. He was naturally Unborn. Man was the mind clothed in matter. He did not have a mind. He was mind. Dualism was not present at first. His kingdom was undisputed. So what of the Spirit?

God, the infinite, incomprehensible cause of all things is spirit. His spirit is the field where all things exist. So His spirit is present in us. It does not rule over us, as a matter of course. We are directed by the free use of our will. It is because His spirit is present that we can discern that He is. If we experience ourselves as we truly are, we are Mind moving over the face of matter, just as God moved over the deep as He contemplated the creation. Should He choose to appear, the spirit being meets us face to face through the medium of flesh and blood. It is a spiritual connection. We have only to bow, that is, we have only to lay down our own crown and acknowledge the spiritual king to feel the majesty and power of His presence. Both spiritual being and mental being can use the body. The human body is designed to provide accommodation for both spirit and mind. In our present condition, the mind is divided. It may uplift its own knowledge as intellect and war against the encroaching unknown, which is spirit.

The Bible tells us that Lucifer was not satisfied with his high office in heaven. He plotted to overthrow the ruler of heaven and take His place. He felt he could do this because he was popular and he judged the Lord by appearance. He could only strike at illusion because if you see the Lord, you do not see the Lord. You simply admire an appearance, an apparition. As humans, we have followed Lucifer's lead. We know what we know, we see what we see. We may think ourselves so wise that we do not seek to understand the nature of our being; we interpret and force our thoughts on the truth. By so doing, we deny the power of the spirit, which is truly absolute. It embraces all things. It predates the existence of your body and sentient mind. By blocking the input of the Creator who desires to interface with His prized creation, we opt to live in tents instead of the mansions of the soul, as author Gina Cerminara called it. God/Holy Spirit is the teacher of men. When we become too knowing, too vain to yield, we lose. There are no adequate words to describe the joy and expansion of life arising from realization of soul.

There is no comparison between having a soul, even a "saved" soul, that is, a soul immersed in the forgiving spirit of God, and being that soul outright. To slip out of the carnal trap is a greater prize than mere heaven, and the fruits begin the moment it occurs. This "it" is enlightenment, illumination, being hit over the head with a spiritual lightning bolt. If you understood, you will stick a lightning rod through your intellect and stand outside during an electric storm. If heaven was the original estate of man, why would Jesus Christ speak of "preparing a place," so that "where I am, you can be also"? If heaven was the proper destination of man, wouldn't a place already be waiting for his return? To prepare a place says, loud and clear, that heaven was not originally designed to accommodate man. Guestrooms had to be built, in a manner of speaking.

XIII

What Is Man? (Part II)

When the question of what man is, is raised, it is customarily approached scientifically, philosophically, and culturally, using thought as the tool of discovery. The answers to the question—what is man?—are superimposed on your consciousness. The answers and ideas conveyed with a degree of authority by the Others produce a gestalt by which we review ourselves and those around us. As the apostle Paul said, "We see through a glass darkly."

We may barely see through the glass, but we tend to take that view as a true impression of the world. We may never have a clue of the contradiction between what we see and what is, unless we are exposed to a fresh experience. A glass or window is a partition between what is outside and what is within. Though it may appear clear, it still distorts the view, as it provides a framed reference that is not present in reality. When we look through a window, we look in a direction preordained by the architect. The choices we have from within the house looking out have been planned for us. It is not much different looking in. We see only as far as the design or plan allows. To get a true picture of the interior, you must enter the door and explore. To truly know what is outside, you must exit through the door.

It is the Tathagatha's ability to walk among men as one of them with the mind of the Unborn (No-Mind), which is the bridge between the shores. There is a probe on earth linked by a satellite in space. The probe sends back data gathered from the third planet about the inhabitants and their ways. The satellite communicates to the probe, keeping it on course. An unknown intelligence guides the satellite, sending data, allowing for constant upgrades to the probe. The probe is able to download the data to any inhabitant who finds it and discovers the password that will unlock its computer. In this manner, the probe, the satellite, and the Unknown Intelligence function as one. With the proper download, the inhabitant of earth can also be brought online with the higher connection.

The chosen teachers are just so. They are what they are and simply grow into their mission. The world cannot dictate their path or understand them because they are not of this world in the truest sense: "in the world but not of the world." Only the Source can fix a flaw that originates in the consciousness of beings. Those who are born in or into the lineage of gurus, Zen masters, sons and daughters of mankind, are the instruments by which this is done. It is not a thing that can be forced even on those who need it. You and all human beings have the great treasure of free will. You must ask for help, then you must follow the teachings of those who answer that call. If you knew the answer, you would not be confused. If you knew how they should teach, they would not be needed.

One of the first things I learned as a student of the Way is the importance of dropping all preconceived notions about what the Way is. Every such notion is a figment of the mind. The notions are simply wrong no matter how true they sound. I had to learn that the guru was present to lead me to the place of awakening. He appears for my benefit alone. Thousands of people may appear to be sitting around him, but the guru sees, hears, and speaks only to the spirit yearning to be free at all cost. Everyone else may simply be entertained by the novelty of his talk, the exotic presence of the white-robed spiritual prince. If you do not experience the singular purpose of the one you call your teacher, you might as well go to a professor and receive college credit for your religious studies. Then your time will not be totally wasted.

You are a single incident of consciousness. You are not me. I am not you. When the guru is talking to me, he is not talking to you. You will not hear the message meant for me. I will not hear the message meant for you.

Sometimes people tell me how someone will come up to them in church after a sermon and tell them what to think of and how to respond to that sermon. That person would go on to tell them what their mission is. When that happens to me, I respond, "That's odd. I was just speaking with God recently and He did not mention that. Are you sure it is not meant for you?"

Be sure. The roshi or guru is only speaking to you. If you would wake up from this dream/nightmare, focus on just one point at a time. Then let everything else fade away. Do not seek it again. Truth always returns on its own.

XIV

Dominion over the Earth: Mind over Matter

September 2005. Hurricane Katrina is ripping through the South, nearly washing away all of the historic city of New Orleans, causing hundreds of deaths, leaving thousands of people homeless, and leaving a wasteland in its wake.

As I contemplated the news, I thought again of Bharati, Guruji's beloved disciple from the temple in Norfolk, Virginia. She, like Guru Rama Mata, was called Mother. We never lost contact through the years. I knew she directed the Freedman's Farm in Furman, Alabama. It is dedicated to teaching youth about nature and conserving the resources of the earth. She was in the path of the hurricane, so I called her. As we discussed the weather conditions, she reflected, "When will man learn to respect the Earth? She is angry." She asked me what I was working on.

I told her I was exploring the transition of man from carnal nature to soul. "If we could but learn to communicate soul to soul, the problems that separate us would fall away," I said.

"It seems so simple," she responded.

"It is simple, but that changes when you try to pass that understanding on to others," I said.

Bharati was given that name by Sadguru Sant Keshavadas. Her legal name is Ellen O. Byrd. She used her time with Guruji to cultivate great resolve, energy, and faith in her own mission. She is a dynamo of activity. I asked her what her plans were regarding Katrina.

"I will just sit it out," she said.

"I will sit with you," I said, speaking with absolute faith that it mattered.

"Thank you," she said, acknowledging that it was so, both spoken and done.

Though separated physically by hundreds of miles we were both comforted knowing that no matter how it appeared, she would not be alone when the wind whipped though the trees.

Bharati spoke of something else that was disturbing her. "A woman told me I was bound for hell because I do not go to church as she does. Why do people think they know your relationship with God?"

"One of the first things we learn in Judeo-Christianity is that God is omnipresent. He is everywhere. Yet, there are many people who confuse their love of ritual worship and place, with God Himself," I explained.

I encountered such thoughts often. I grew up in the church. I understand its spirit as the "Universal Church." I understand the contradictions that arise out of the confused thoughts of men. I was blessed with a special blessing, one that is often much like a curse in many ways. I know the taste of ALONENESS. Long before I knew anything, long before I began the quest for realization, I lived in mushin, in the aliveness of No-Mind. It is because I fell from that state of grace, and labored to return to it, that I understand the absence of realization.

Zen master Bankei warns the Zen practitioner that we can exchange the "marvelously illuminating Buddha Mind for that of a demon." I bear witness that it is so. Without my having fallen into despair and turmoil, however, my life would have benefited no one but myself. I would have had no clue to what other people felt. How can there be empathy for conditions you cannot even imagine?

I am aware now that the only way I can write and teach Dharma is to have lived the life I have. Insights into our fundamental nature arise only when we are apart from that truth. We can only help someone else when we understand what he or she feels. We can guide that person across the mind's treacherous field only when we have passed through the worst and returned to our Original Home. There is no formula to give to you. What helps is a true telling of the journey, the recounting of an adventure spun not by the intellect but the soul. Using words, experiences, actions, and nonactions, dedicated to drenching you with the wetness from the still waters of the Mind, I endeavor to inspire you to drink the essence of spiritual awakening.

XV

You Are Not the Body

Without faith, you cannot go through the Door that leads to an enlightenment, your realization of who and what you really are. The inner path or Zen, as we refer to it here, is a direct pointing at the soul. The key word is DIRECT.

Scholars pursue facts, students apply themselves to lessons, but a disciple mirrors his master. He believes that he is what he projects himself to be. He believes that the master is endowed with authority by the supreme authority. He accepts that the master is ordained by the Holy Spirit to do what he does. Thus the disciple humbles himself, and places faith in the master as instrument and the teachings of the master as the Way. It is because of this unique Guru-chela (Master-disciple) relationship that the master speaks freely. There is no conflict or duality, no doubt when he responds and expresses the Way to those who come to him. If you believe the teacher is true, you must cast aside your intellect and listen to what he teaches. You must act as if his words are unimpeachable if they are to do their work.

When Sadguru Sant Keshavadas said, "You are not the body," I knew in that instant that what he said was true. From that moment, I recognized that I was not the body, yet I still carried the carcass everywhere I went in my waking hours, dragging it from room to room. Although I was not the body, something or someone was holding it up and sitting it down. Someone was using it to receive signals and impressions from and of the Earth. Who received this data? If this mystery being, this "self," was not of flesh and blood, what was it, and where did it reside?

> And be not conformed to this world: but be ye transformed by the renewing of your mind, that ye may prove what is that good, and acceptable, and perfect, will of God. (Rom. 12:2)

One day Guruji called to me. I sat at his feet while he gave me a hard lesson. I had the enlightenment experience of a Zen warrior. There was passion and fire in my soul, not only for the damage done to my ancestors and those of my culture living today, but also for the harm done to me. As a poet/activist/warrior, I boldly faced challenges and fought for the downtrodden. In 1969, I was arrested with the Queens College 39 in a major event that initially involved 300 students and 500 tactical police officers armed with rifles and shields. In the end, 38 students and one faculty member were arrested in a protest against the lack of student rights. Of the people arrested, I was the lone African-American.

Although the college boasted a Black and Puerto Rican Coalition, a militant group, they refused to bail me out of jail. Everyone knew me because of my newspaper column, "Meditation," and poetic activity. The militant leadership voted, however, to ignore my plight because I was arrested with white student protestors. There had been at least 50 or more African-American students involved in the takeover of the social science building, but I was the only one who stayed. In truth, I was not a protestor. I was assigned to cover the story from the inside by Talib Zobeir of *Etcetera* magazine, an African-American journal of letters. I got too close to the story.

Months later, we were sentenced to 15 days in jail on Rikers Island during summer vacation. All of the other students were white and Jewish middle class. When we arrived, we were interviewed by the *New York Times* and the *Daily Press*. I was isolated from the rest.

I was taken to the basement where I was interrogated. My father taught that a warrior only gives his name, rank, and serial number. I only had a name. I told them nothing about the leadership of the protest, which happened to be under the umbrella of the Students for a Democratic Society. The officers struck me repeatedly in the face, but I did not speak. I relaxed and entered my secret place. Frustrated by my seemingly impervious nature in the face of pain, the office balled his fist and aimed it for my face. In that instance, I blocked and struck. Another officer leaped, and I caught him with a kick. Realizing what was happening, I threw up my hands and apologized. "I did not mean to respond that way. You should have warned me," I said. "I am a martial artist."

The apology was not accepted. Suddenly more policemen rushed in. I felt something building within me like a great wave, a tsunami of the Spirit. I knew that I could kill them all without effort. I also knew what I must do. I yielded my body and took the blows; I yielded my mind. In moments, I was gone away into some indefinable space that admitted no light, but I could hear everything. I heard the screaming, the sound of the blows, but I had no body to feel them. I was present, but I had no form to discern. Then I heard a voice say, "We killed him." There was silence. Out of this vacuum came a rushing wind. I was back in my body, standing, feeling strong. The cops jumped back in alarm. "That was a good workout," I said pretentiously.

I felt no pain. When they led me back up from the basement, things turned worse. The captain of Cell Block 13 looked at me and said, "I heard what you did in there. Bow your head and shuffle your feet or I will order these cops to break both of your legs." Dad taught me that a warrior always chooses death before dishonor. I clenched my fist, prepared to take as many of them with me as I could before they shot me dead.

Suddenly, there was a black officer at my ear. "I know you have great courage, but you have no friends in here. Please do what they say or they will make me participate. Submit," he said.

That one word, submit, was my salvation. An Islamic mystic named Robert C13X had told me the importance of submitting to the will of the Supreme. Before Nomura Roshi, long before I met Sadguru Sant Keshavas, I met Robert in Lenny's Book N Things in Brooklyn. This was in 1965, when I was 17 years old. He said without introduction or hesitation, "You have the Divine Mind," then he endeavored to prove that it was so. He asked me to fast for two weeks, then invited me to Mosque

7C in Brooklyn, after buying me dinner to break the fast at a restaurant then known as Burger King, an establishment not related to the chain.

What happened would only be echoed by spiritual teachers from many cultures. There was no place to hide, but I tried to run anyway.

Guruji praised my attainment, but he told me he felt the anger coiled beneath the surface. He was right.

The police captain commanded that I do the one thing I vowed never to do, to dishonor myself and my ancestors. The African-American police officer complicated things. He appealed to me to save him from dishonoring himself. I bowed my head and shuffled my feet. When I was in the cell, I clenched my fist so hard that I could not open my hand for days and I fell to the cot, crying with great passion. For the first time in my life, I knew hate. I wanted to destroy those who had denied my identity and tried to force on me a lie called the nigger, as they kicked and pounded and screamed with venom, "nigger-nigger-nigger." I longed to spill the blood of my unrepentant enemy. I was a warrior, no less than King David, no less than Joshua, no less than Samson. Did black skin designate the only tribe in the history of the world who had no right to defend against its enemies?

Guruji named me for Krishna. The first name he gave me was Krishnadas, indicating that I served the Lord manifesting as warrior/friend/lover. Surely, he would understand what I felt.

"I want you to volunteer your time to the police department," he said. My blood pressure shot up dangerously, but I was respectful. I obeyed.

By being obedient to Father God speaking through the guru, I not only lost my hatred of police as a generic order, but I also found wonderful new friends who wore badges and rekindled a long-time friendship with Police Sergeant, later, Lieutenant, Charles O. Neal, a master of Jujitsu and a Judo teacher who had influenced me early in life. His office in Crime Prevention became my office away from my own. We teamed up and accomplished many wonderful things together. It was through the efforts of Master Neal that my Zen insights into Bushido were translated into legitimate martial arts dan (black belt) rank.

The word of the guru penetrated to the marrow of the problem and opened new doors because I was obedient. My ego was opposed to the order, but the disciple must yield to the master if he is to benefit from the wisdom of the master. There is no alternative to obedience. Skillful means, upaya, is not something you need to understand. You must exercise faith because the master will throw curves to the ego that it cannot catch.

Lord Jesus forbids disciples to conform their minds to what can be seen in this world. That leaves nothing for the mind to cling to. It is not to abide in form. He adds that the disciple must be transformed in a familiar teaching, by the renewing of the mind. This is precisely what the historical Buddha taught a half-millennium before. This does not give bragging rights to Buddhists, however, as you will see. What it underscores is the nature of the working of Holy Spirit/Universal Mind through the ages. There are things that we must do, ourselves, to break free. A strong swimmer can dive into rough water and save a drowning man. Being saved does not make the rescued worthy of the honor of the hero who dove into the deep to save him. If that man would grow to be able to help others, he must apply himself to learning how to swim and rescue others. He must exert his own will to transform that which is within his own realm of authority.

This is the line separating the inner path from the outer. The inner path leads to mastery because the disciple struggles and works toward that goal by utilizing the tools revealed to him and the power of his own will to strengthen his spirit. A strong spirit ascends to mastery over body and mind. Light penetrates darkness.

The outer path is centered on the Lord Incarnate. He is the primary object of faith. The worshipper who focuses on the human manifestation of his Lord cannot go beyond him. That Lord is always Lord and Master. To take the inner path is to move into the realm of spirit. Spirit communes with spirit as two bodies of water flow one into the other.

As the disciple embraces the Spirit, he flows to the same point of focus as the Lord Incarnate. His concentration has no content, no image. When the disciple can live as spirit, his body becomes the temple of the Lord/Father. When he receives Original Mind, he is without duality; he is a Buddha, that is, he stands in the position of son also. He is free. Buddha is not the Almighty. Buddha is man mirroring the nature of God. This is what the Scriptures declare is the essence of man. The Book of Genesis declares:

> In the likeness of God created He him, male and female created He them.

Words are fashioned only for a feeling, understanding, thought, object, or experience we desire to share with another person. Where there is no thought or experience, there is no word to point to it. The word "Buddha" exists in Asia because the experience of enlightenment, the return to our root consciousness has been recorded for millenniums. In the West, European thinkers approached the world as an object outside the mind. Thought was the missile sent to explore the universe and all that could be found in it by the senses. The probing device for all inquiry, secular and spiritual, was the mind. This presented a major barrier to the transformation promised by Christ. While Christianity is the primary spiritual tradition of the Western world, it is still a product of the East. Men were admonished to surrender their minds, to give up thought to become instruments of the Father. Instead of discovering the Light of the World, the Incarnate Lord, the Western church entered a practice of adhering to the "body" of the teachings, the vessel of transformation. This exercise produced a religious mind that valued thoughts about spiritual views and ideas over the sovereignty of the Spirit. The spoken word took a high seat, a place of honor that should have been reserved for the silently illuminating personal connection provided by the Word. As Jesus illustrated by his parable on the missing sheep, the Lord values the one. He will surely seek you out, if you cry out.

In another parable, Jesus speaks of the prodigal son. A wealthy man has one son who stays with him, but he pines for the son who ran away into the world. He sends the faithful son in search of the lost offspring. Though the lost one returns feeling unworthy and alien to his surroundings, the father treats him with great honor. He is a prince in the eyes of his sire. He has returned home to the love of his father. All is forgiven.

I do not see the Scriptures as words to be debated like literature in English class. If we debate on whose interpretation is correct, we miss an important lesson the Scriptures teach. We are to rightly divide the word of truth. I cannot nourish your body by consuming food for you. If you receive understanding from the Scriptures by meditating on them, there is a lesson, a message there, that is for you alone. No matter how brilliant your insight, it will not take you as far as what you glean from your own faith approach, your own personal meditation. To me, the Scriptures are like the Kigan koans of Zen. They are an interlocking mystery that opens its secrets to those who seek in all sincerity to be illumined by the message God is sending. To me, He is speaking to only one person, the searching soul. If I am he, He spins the cosmos to help me discover the code that will free my mind and release my soul of its prison. If you are that searching soul, the universe has just turned in your direction. No two people get the same message because there is, in fact, nothing to retain by rote. There are keys that will set you free. When you uncover them, put them in the locks and turn. When the lights come on, the "fatted calf" is slain in your honor.

> I and the Father are one. I would ye be one also.
>
> —Jesus of Nazareth

Traditionally, as the very name of our religion indicates, Christians embrace Christ as Lord. This is a good thing. There is no problem with Jesus Christ himself. There is a huge problem with those who labor under his name without taking time to "listen" to him and find out for themselves why he took the route of sacrifice for mankind. I say that he took the path of sacrifice for mankind, and not just Christians, for the simple reason that that was the purpose. The defining and limiting term "Christian" was not a name bestowed on the disciples of Jesus by Jesus. His disciples, like him, were charged to go out into the world to teach and preach all he had taught them. The names they were called then were Peter, Paul, John, James, and so on. They were charged to go forth as individuals (as in undivided or single-minded) filled with the Holy Spirit to uplift humanity.

Since the Spirit of God was part of mankind in the beginning of the Earth experience, the indication was that now restoration was possible. If we are true to the original understanding, only those who are Christlike would be called Christians, for that is what was meant when the name was first used at Antioch. It is not a designation for people who claim membership in a particular church.

The sixth chapter of the Book of Genesis tells us that God was so dissatisfied with the deeds of man that His spirit would not strive with our kind much longer. The moment God ceased abiding or inhabiting man we became disconnected from Source. Our Source is the Spirit of God, the essence of our being. The material universe provides the substance. The motive power and awareness of our existence stems from Mind. Focused on the body, it responds to the data supplied by the five senses using learned behavior and innate understanding inherent in our nature. This constitutes a sentient being. When mind embraces spirit, mankind accommodates its daily life to the Way of the Spirit. This is not a statement of religion but of nature. The mind that lives through the flesh is, for all purposes, flesh and blood. The mind that knows itself through the medium of spirit experiences itself as spirit. When this happens the person becomes, once again, "a living soul."

The purpose of Zen is to awaken flesh and blood beings to their spiritual centers. Since Zen training is to teach a soul how to live and prosper on Earth again, it can hardly be counter to God's original schematic of what man is. Both God and man walked the gardens of Eden. Both God and man conversed through the vehicle of bodies. Both God and man were invisible beings enjoying a visual and tactile encounter. Both God and man acted singularly, of one, independent mind. The First Man did not hesitate to voice his own opinion or ideas to God. God did not hesitate to consider the validity of what man said.

If you are inclined toward what can be proven in the laboratory by scientists or scholars, you are not on the path of faith. Your path is different and built on proof in this world. Gospel/Dharma, any teaching that arises out of God or his designates, must be accepted as immutable truth on its face, proof or not. You use your five senses to understand things, but those senses are attached to an impermanent body in a world you one day found yourself in.

Spiritual truth arises from a different dimension than what is revealed to your bodily senses. If you decide this moment to accept that the Scriptures are true, you will need no outside proof to experience the power that simple decision will have on you. So here is the fact. Once upon a time, God and man sat around the fire and chatted for the sheer camaraderie of it all. How does an invisible and unfathomable being carry on a conversation with a human being? He meets him on common ground. He fashions a garment of dust for Himself to match the one worn by man and comes in on the spiritual network. After all, the mental being, man (*manu* in Sanskrit), is spirit at the core of his physical being. Spirit communes with spirit, not flesh.

As we live our lives in the daily world, soul is a prisoner and slave. It lives in a prison disguised to appear as self. The mind was used to lock us in darkness, and the mind must be used to break free. Realization is not a gift. You must consciously, willfully, strike out on the quest, armed only with faith in the unknown. You are not the body. Accept this observation from those who have tested it. If you accept this truth, you will have made an important decision. You life will change from this moment. You are not the body, so what is it in relation to what you really are? As we continue this meditation, you will come to feel the answer to this question.

The path to awakening cannot be mere theory or belief. If that were so, every religious person and scholar would be enlightened. Zen is direct. There are no intermediaries allowed in such a mind. All barriers must be broken through to free the soul to be its own glorious self. What helped me along the way, and what will help you, is not mere discourse but the sincere utterances of those who made the connection. Only their sayings have power to get you through the gate. That is so because they speak from the other side of that gate, not from the world, peering upward to get a glimpse of it.

I share my experiences with you freely when I believe that such sharing will help you have faith in your own mission of freedom. You may ask, who is he to dare speak to such a topic when there are so many great teachers of the past who can help us? Well, there are many great teachers of the past. You can ask them nothing new. Guruji told me, "Only a living guru can initiate a disciple." If one does not have the initiation during his lifetime, it will be too late. While the teachings are universal, all illuminated masters penetrate the same One Truth. The spirit of the teacher and the mind of the teacher radiate from generation after generation, adding new personality and immediacy to the message. The nature of water does not change, but the glass that contains it can look and feel as different as the imagination of the designer. No one can drink the glass itself, but they reach for the glass anyway. If you want to drink, you will go where the chilled glass of sparkling, shimmering life is. It has lost none of its life-giving virtue in this vessel.

Who would dare say, "I am the Way"? What man would be bold enough to declare, "In the heavens above and the earth below, I, alone am the most honored one"? I had the strangest feeling that man was in my mirror. Could be, he is in yours, too. Does that make you nervous or excited? Relax. If you think about it, you will only fall off course. It is not necessary to have a strong intellect, nor is it necessary to be able to articulate your experience to others to awaken. How much thought did you give to being born? Did you plan how to react when the hand of the doctor introduced you to the world with a cold slap across your naked butt? The hand struck. You cried out. Perfect response.

Of course, the Great Master is in my mirror. The Scriptures uphold that understanding.

> Bible: He who is within [me] is greater than he who is in the world.

> Zen: All men are buddhas. It is like ice and water. Apart from water no ice can exist. Apart from men there can be no buddhas.

It is a question of belief versus faith. Do you believe enough to abandon the appearance of things and stand naked in the teachings? Only those who abandon the discursive thoughts of the ego mind, thus the illusion body, will be transformed by the truth. There is no manipulating the outcome. There is just this moment when you realize you are about to die. There is this nanosecond to choose to live or die. If you choose to pull back and live, you have chosen to continue dying in linear time. Only those who drop their body and mind, only those who choose to willingly enter this dark place on faith, to be annihilated by the One, will find eternal life on the other side of the experience, in this world, right here, right now. The proposition is frightening. That is why there is no substitute for faith. You must believe that there is someone, someone benevolent waiting to receive you on the other side of the "wormhole" of inner space. All that we have is the testimony of those we believe have made the leap.

All we have is their mind-map to the "gateless-gate." So what do we do to make it happen?

> Flint strikes steel . . . a spark!
>
> —Zen saying

The perfect act comes without mediation or hesitation.

The flint is in the visible world. The steel is in the visible world. Until the moment of the strike, there is no spark. When you do all that you can and can go no further, there is still activity. It originates beyond your mind and the realm of sight and sound. You are used to believing in the known factors. To return to your Original Nature where you live as soul in this world, where you communicate soul to soul, you must place your faith in X.

You must believe in the immeasurable power and intelligence of the X-Factor.

You can exert no control over X. You can only trust the veracity of its input and guidance from the moment you agree to be initiated. In the schools of this world, you depend on your ability to learn and know. In this school, all depends on your ability to empty your mind of what you know, then drop even that mind.

"What are you carrying?
"A staff."
"Drop it!"
The staff clatters to the floor.
"Drop it!" the Zen master yells.
"I have nothing," the monk responds.
"Drop it!" the Zen master yells.

I do not question your intelligence. You are reading this far, so it is clear you have an inquiring mind and are of above-average intelligence, but that will not help you any further than to whet your appetite for an experience no mere words or concepts of any kind can bring about. Thus it is important that I emphasize that what you are seeking lies between the words. What you are seeking is coming to you now from my mind to your mind. Listen with your mind. Do not listen for the sound of my voice. I am saying nothing. Listen! Only listen. Listening will create a vacuum. There is something that belongs in that emptiness that cannot be obtained in time and space.

This state of listening samadhi is like Telstar, that lonely satellite pointed into deep space, waiting on the one signal that will substantiate the value of its existence. One day, the signal, the spark will come. On that day the lights will truly come on in the house of love. The song "House of Love," by Vince Gill and Amy Grant, always inspired the feeling in me of the human soul illuminated. It only happens one person at a time. Religion is a collective spiritual practice. It is like a train. The engineer does all the driving and everyone aboard heads for the same destination. In Christianity, the train leads to Jesus' house, to his mansion.

> In my Father's house there are many mansions. If it were not so, I would have told you.
>
> —Jesus

To be sure, Jesus' house must be a wonderful place, but what about those other mansions? Who lives in those? How does one get a contract on the place across the street or down the road? Well, the answer to that question is written in the Book.

Jesus tells his disciples that it is the Father who dispenses crowns (honors). It is the Father, alone, not Jesus, who determines who will sit on the throne next to Jesus. It is this power, the power behind the authority of Jesus that awards "Mansions of the Soul." Jesus Christ did not have an ego problem. That affliction is suffered by his later followers. He clearly indicated that a disciple could go through him to connect with the Father. The question comes to mind, if you take that route, to seek the Father for yourself, "who's your daddy?"

> Jesus: A double-mind is unstable in all of its ways.

> Zen: Above all don't wobble.

It is said that we are born innocent. It is also said that we are born in sin. Which statement is true? The enlightened ones say, "The conflict between good and evil is the disease of the mind."

All are true. Innocence is born into a form separated (sin) from the source of its origin. The more it identifies with form, the deeper it sinks into the sin/separated nature. By a certain age, innocence is blocked and consciousness is caught by the world of form. The Original or natural relationship with our being or Creator is to simply be in Him without thought. It is the Way of our being. We can say that the inner path is not a path when we are born, but simply the truth of our nature expressed. To return is possible so long as we do not completely lose our *INNER SENSE.*

If we lose our innocence (inner sense), the only way to reconnect is from a different perspective. We are led from outside. The Light of the World, the Word Manifest, comes to us through a person to lead us. Those who maintain an intuitive sense of their Original Home are able to take the accelerated course. Such a course transcends the world and operates in the dimension of spirit and Original Mind one on one. If you are still reading, and feeling a sense of connection to what I am conveying, you are being led to the inner path. One day you will meet your teacher.

XVI

Son of Man/Son of God: Brothers of the Blood

In the James Bond movie *For Your Eyes Only*, the theme song contains these words: "For your eyes only, for only your eyes see me through the night."

At Soul Sword Zen Institute, I teach students and disciples of the Way that, once you are initiated or accept the Truth, there is a greater reality than apparent to the senses. You become the student of the Great Master, the JagadGuru, the Word, the Holy Spirit. As such, the teacher who is the eternal guru without form can reach you through any form or means. You must remain aware. When you practice spiritual awareness, that is, mindfulness of the unknown and unexpected, you will not only be able to sense problems, but also recognize when you are being taught.

To be "chosen" means you have no choice as regards the mission of your life; but you do have a will. A will gives you plenty of room for wandering off that unknown course, but you cannot run from what you cannot see or may not even suspect. So running wild and free is like a child believing the playpen is the world. No matter what side of the pen you're on, no matter where you hide, mother will find you, father will find you.

Zen, or enlightenment, is solely direct experience. Only the direct experience, only the message that comes uncensored and unedited from the essence of the awakened ones can help you. If it stems from the intellect, it will serve only the intellect. It may entertain you, the words may educate and amaze you, but they will no more wake you up to the truth of your being than someone in a dream throwing a bucket of water on your sleeping dream body.

So what we call the path of the masters unfolds backward. Like the afterburner of a passing jet, the mark appears on the path after the plane is gone.

What helped me, what continues to help me, are the lights shining in the darkness. They are the masters who came before. They may have come before me on the time line, but they stand ahead of me in reality. Their beacon leads me from light to light, but their lives once lived in the flesh are the lamps on which those brilliant bulbs stand. If they were perfect in every way from the beginning of their lives, they would be useless to me, and to you. It is their humanness that gives hope. When a man born of woman from the seed of man can penetrate heaven and shine as a star among stars, that is reassuring. There lies hope for us all. A master, an enlightened one, is but an ordinary man turned inside out. Perhaps right-side-up would also be a good phrase. We have functioned upside down for centuries. The perspective gained from a life standing on your head is flawed.

Christians focus on Jesus as the Son of God. Yet he was first called the Son of Man. The sequence is significant. It was when the Holy Spirit of God merged with the Son of Man that man became the Son of God. God needed a representative man to work his plan. The Son of Man loves his father(s) and the Son of God loves his Father. The Original Man, that is, the First Adam and the Second Adam, is akin to a file transfer after an upgrade on your computer. There is a sense of familiarity in the midst of newness. Jesus Christ, the Second Adam, is the cable hookup that permits the operation of a vast spiritual network. Suddenly, man, who was offline since the introduction of a local virus to his system, is back online and able to access the Web with ease. The network, up and running, can and must now be utilized. The Network must be alive for it to work for living beings. Thus the Son of Man and the Son of God are complementary to each other. As it takes both yin and yang to establish harmony, it takes two versions of the One to communicate.

If there is a message to be sent, there must be someone to receive it. The sender is not the receiver; the receiver is not the sender. The message, the Word, is apart from He who transmits. The Word, the active spirit or power of God, is also alive, one with the total, but yet not quite the same. The Son of Man is singular. The term signifies a type. Conversely, man, as the Sanskrit term for us underscores, man is translated as *manu*, a mental being. The power of our uniqueness is the mind. While this is the fundamental truth, we do not experience it. Ordinary people have a mind. Manu is Mind. The man of the beginning was the Living Mind. In this context, the Son of Man would be translated as the Son of the Mind, the Son of the Original or Universal Mind.

As frightening as it may sound from a strictly religious sense, man, void of all other labels and concepts, is none other than Buddha. By this I do not mean a Buddhist. The word is used as it was meant to be understood . . . AWAKE, MIND. If we are awake, we have no need of any religion because we cannot be awake and lost in darkness at the same time. To be awake is to be alive in Truth, to see things as they really are, to live through, in, and by God, by nature. If this is so, there can be no God outside the experience of living. Life is seamless. It is written: "In Him we move and have our being."

Christ wore a seamless robe to the crucifixion. Later, the Romans, who laid the foundation for Western Civilization, tore the one robe into two pieces. Meditate on this.

To believe that we live and have our being in God is marvelous; indeed, to experience it brings incomprehensible and never-ending joy and awe at the expanding glory of the Universe and *that* which forever lies behind our vision. The incredible current of life and love that lifts you ever higher and higher is a vibration of bliss and wisdom throughout your being, a being that has no locality and no duality. You can only experience this alone. If you are not the Son of Man, yourself, this door is closed to you at present. This is not a secondary experience. It is not a crown you want on the head of someone else. To desire that is to fail your own eternal Father. He has but One True Son, One True Daughter on Earth. The Celestial Son clothes himself in flesh to reach out to the falling Terrestrial Son. To know your Father is to hear His voice calling out, "Turn," and somersault though fathomless inner space no matter how long it takes or how hard it is, knowing, believing, holding faith that your brother is out there somewhere hanging upside down, swinging out to meet you among the stars . . . one day he will catch you and stop your fall. He will fling you higher and higher and you will let go again to tumble through the void alone to the one who brought your life forth from nothing but Himself.

The Son of God/the Son of Man? They are linked to a purpose beyond comprehension. They are eternally linked with and inseparable from each other, yet the left hand is not likely to know what the right hand is doing. To qualify as a Son according to the example set by Jesus, one must surrender one's will to the Father, so as to become the sailing vessel guided by His spirit. It is the Father who guides the actions and speaks the words attributed to the Son. The Son must remain faithful to the Father by *not* relying on his own understanding. He must never lose sight of the primary mission for which he lives, to do the will of the Father.

To say or believe that one KNOWS the will of the Father suggests that everything is mapped out and fixed like the geography of the world. To DO the will of the father is not dualistic. When Jesus said, "I and the Father are one," it fit perfectly with the statement, "When you have seen me, you have seen the Father."

What is the will of the Father? Ask a newborn baby, one second after he enters the world of consciousness. You will get the perfect answer. No singular being knows it all, even if he is one with He who does. It is said clearly that Jesus does not know the day or the hour when he will return. I always find it interesting that so many other people think they do know.

In the beginning, you were declared a living soul. What are you now? As a living soul, you were one with the Spirit. There is no way to KNOW what this is. The only truth is to become that again.

That does not sound like a being that can be bound by anything of this world. A meditating Zen monk was threatened by a Mongolian warrior wielding a sword over him. He recited a verse spontaneously:

> In heaven and earth no crack to hide,
> Joy to know that man is void and the things too are void,
> Splendid the great Mongolian long sword,
> Its lightning flash cuts the spring breeze.

Zen master Bukko did not tremble before the sword held over him because from where he sat there was nothing and no one to be killed. This may be hard to understand from the position of one still living in carnal mind.

In the early 1960s, before I had heard the word "Zen," I saw a newsreel at the movies in which a monk who was protesting the Vietnam War doused himself in gasoline and set himself afire. It should have been a horrible scene because the camera did not turn away. It wasn't. The monk sat in the midst of the flames in lotus posture, his hands folded in prayer. He sat that way for a long time, then his body fell. In a magnificent effort, he composed himself again in the flames. There he sat until there was no one left to sit.

"What manner of man can do this?" I thought aloud. I wanted such resolve, such courage. I remembered the words of the apostle Paul, "Though I give my body to be burned, have I not love, I am but a tingling brass." The Buddhist monk gave himself for the cause of peace and love. I was a Christian Sunday School teacher at the time, yet my spirit identified with his great sacrifice. Later, more of his brothers did the same. That they could do such a thing without making a sound told me something I heard in the inmost depths of my being.

The wind does not flinch when swords and spears pierce through its space. Who cries? It is just this person you must find and kill yourself. It is the illusion of there being a self to die that is the root of what we call sin, separation from God.

"I am come that ye might have life and have it more abundantly," said Jesus Christ. There is no death in life. There is no life in death. It is like the Zen example of wood and ashes. Wood is just wood. The consuming fire produces ashes, but there is no wood in ashes. If you believe in "abundant life, eternal life," if you recognize that life is a product of Spirit, you must appreciate by faith that there can be no end to that life if you have already merged with Spirit. What persists is the dualistic mind that clings to the memories and fears of the carnal state. Where there is strong doubt, the mind wobbles.

The Sons of Man function as beings anchored in the original truth of their nature. They are Tathagathas. From their perspective, their activity in the world is like a reflection in a mirror. Actions arise unimpeded.

They leave no trace. The Tathagatha is unborn. Perhaps it would help to say that one is a Tathagatha when the originating spirit of man rules the mind/body. The link with eternity, with timelessness, is never severed. He simply steps into the stream of time. He is never carried away by it into the world.

This view is supported by the patriarchs who, in providing help for those who are passing through the ranks of enlightenment, say the following of the Real.

> Within nothing there is a path
> Leading away from the dust of this world.
>
> —Tōzan's Ryōkai's "Verses on the Five Ranks"
> (quoted in *The Zen Koan,* by Isshū Miura
> and Ruth Fuller Sasaki)

> For God so loved the world that he gave His only begotten son that whosoever believed in him should not perish but would have eternal life.
>
> —John 3:16

When I first heard that verse of the Bible as a child, I was overjoyed. It was such a relief to learn that we Christians had eternal life. I quickly became confused when I noticed that, despite that verse, there were funerals being held in our church. I was curious. If we had eternal life, who or what was being buried? Why were people grieving?

Preachers preach to human beings. Teachers teach spiritual beings. The role of the preacher is to guide his flock to keep their minds on the Lord, the Author of Salvation. The mission of the teacher is to wake up the soul so that the prodigal sons and daughters can return to their rightful place in the Father while they are still on the Earth. Under the guidance of a spiritual teacher—read guru, roshi, and so on—the spirit ascends to the throne of the mind and man becomes once again a living soul. Without help, soul is ruled by carnal mind. It remains a prisoner of the flesh because it sees the world through the program of a mind that interprets life solely or mostly through the medium of the senses. No religion frees men from their pettiness and divisiveness. Though all major religions preach love, peace, and tolerance, the individual and collective lives of the practitioners do not reflect this higher nature as a matter of course. The practitioners may desire this, they may believe in such virtues, but the sentient mind wars against spirit.

There is an inherent contradiction in the way religion goes about instilling virtues. While Christ dies to his own will and makes himself a willing pawn to the will of the Father, modern believers tend to seek only what they can get out of the relationship. Heaven is not enough. They want material goods, honor, and, whenever possible, an ethnically pure neighborhood. Whereas Christians may profess a love for your soul and seek to get you saved for your own good, it is not a given that they will love you as a human being. This contradiction is possible in all religions because there is a difference between belief and transformation. Those who return to the root of being are connected to the root of all beings; one tree, supported by a root system that spreads throughout the planet. Its branches embrace heaven. One tree, supporting the Son of Man and the Son of God, one tree nourished in the Garden of the Father. How splendid.

To hear the words, to read them, or otherwise engage them with your thoughts will not really help. Thoughts divide your mind from Mind.

To be chosen, then, is to be preordained, to be set aside. In a way, it is like being a cosmic secret agent but the secret is so secure that not even you, the agent, has a clue that anything is happening, not one clue at all until it is time. To be yourself is nothing special. If there is going to be an indication of an anomaly, it will be introduced by someone outside of you. The "norm" is the control group. Extremes are measured against the status quo. When you are just you, your actions, expressions, and feelings are unimpeded. Conformity occurs when there is pressure to act or think like the control group. Among those who do not fit into the norm are geniuses, artists, the mentally impaired, and those with heightened spirituality, among others.

The mind-set referred to as the norm is kept in place by a number of means. One of them is by creating and maintaining laws that, in effect, constitute behavior control. Human beings can be programmed through pain and depravation. The process is known as brainwashing. Given enough time, an expert can have a suspect confessing to the murder of his still very much alive mother. When the mind is focused on the body, it thoroughly identifies with its mortality and vulnerability. When fear can be instilled, almost at will, there is a ready steering mechanism for outside control. Long before you understood the necessity of "mindfulness," skillful infiltrators had begun to guide your mind. You may think your thoughts are your own. You do think in words, don't you? Where did you get the words that you string together to form a view? Who assigned them meaning? For just one moment, consider: What valuable thing do you know for which there is no word?

Zen is a word anyone can use. It is especially helpful because it does not point to dogma or philosophy. Its purpose is not to stimulate your intellect. Zen is your tasting the tea and sensing its heat and wetness for yourself. In the Zen way, you are the lightning bolt, not the observer, you are the thunder shouting. You are that experience. There is no one to pass it along to. You are that man or woman for which the creation exists. See, hear, speak, touch, taste, smell it to the utmost. Consume it! When you have burned the experience into a crisp, then and only then should the reflecting consciousness kick in . . . AHHHHH!

One day you open your eyes for the first time and you cry. A new genius is in the world. The Anointed One and the Enlightened One also entered the world as defenseless infants. Will the light of your mind remain bright or dim? For a while, you are at the mercy of the environment and others. As you lie in the crib, kicking your legs about, the first agent of your downfall comes forward with a smile. Your mother lays you upon her breast and coos. "My baby," she says. "Mother will protect you from everything she can." There is one thing she will miss. She will focus on protecting your body and preparing your mind to enter the world. How can she know she is preparing a soul for sacrifice according to the plan of the Ruler of this World?

How did man the living soul become so easy to manipulate, and why? Who gains from our ignorance of what we are?

It is written in the Bible, "Ye shall know the truth, and the truth shall set you free."

When the chains fall off your mind, they will drop off your body, as well. There is nothing outside in the world that can help you. Help is not to be found in the place or in the face. If you are searching for help, it is time to be quiet and stop the quest. Your prayers have already been heard. Read between the lines; remember, the answer is there in the empty spaces. This is not the kind of battle that can be fought with a large army. You will have but one warrior at your beck and call. That warrior is you. The roshi or guru is a mirror reflecting what you are within. The flow of wisdom and power is circular. If you look deeply, you will recognize yourself. What is the message?"

A friend and fellow disciple of Sadguru Sant Keshavadas expressed concern at how negative the world has become. "We need an invisible army," she said.

"It has always been here. Your reaction to the world is proof you are in that army," I said.

The first and most important act of a spiritual warrior is to slay the demons within. "Physician, heal thyself."

This is not the normal path people take. They get a taste of salvation and then are quick to condemn and disdain others who are on the path they once traveled. There is a lack of compassion, even though many religions probably believe that their militant approach to spreading "the Gospel" or good news of their particular order is motivated by compassion. To desire to help people is a good thing, but beating them down with thoughts is not the same thing as touching them spirit to spirit.

When others experience the presence of life and light within you, they move closer, attracted by what is genuine. The mind can always be manipulated. It can be made to act within a positive frame, just as it can be trained to act against the best interest of a person. The success of slavery was that it made human beings give up their will to other human beings. They did what they did not want to do. Spirituality is to be real. You must not, cannot blindly surrender your soul. When a disciple yields to a spiritual master, he is certain that that master is working in harmony with him to the end of achieving his freedom. It is a relationship, not bondage.

When the dam breaks, the water flows according to its nature, unrestricted by artificial barriers. The forces of the world do not trust in that nature, so they bind your mind early. The Original Man was wise. He was at one with himself. This was his spirituality. There was nothing within him, no obstruction of any kind. When there is nothing to meditate about within you, the only focus of meditation is the seen world. The Earth and the events of each day were the natural meditations of

Original Man. What he did expressed his spirit. There is no need for a formal religion when one is not separate from the Creation or the Creator. In you, the spirit of the Creator becomes a single experience of life in a specific locality. The form divides, but it need not separate you from the cosmic identity, the Allness.

There is religious arrogance, which should not be; neophytes do not know and perhaps do not suspect who they really are. It is dangerous to advancement to seek God or understanding only in a formal, organized setting. It is like stopping at kindergarten when there is a vast endless university accessible to those who direct their faith toward the Unknown, rather than to what is known. If you need the approval and consensus of any group or person to seek deeper, you are limited to their understanding. We advance according to our own faith. The sword must be turned on our own minds in order to cut the enemy out and see clearly. We must cut duality in twain. An ordinary sword cuts in two. The spiritual sword cuts in oneness. It heals the split. We see so much that is wrong about the world before our eyes, but no matter what we do, nothing will change significantly . . . unless . . .

When we learn to seek and destroy the rogue programming in our own mind, we will understand. It is from this place of tacit understanding that we make a difference. One man can make all the difference when he is unified, when he is of one mind and one spirit. When these expressions of the Godhead merge with and function as a human being, anything can happen at any moment.

If you are reading this with your spirit, you will feel a quickening. If that is what you feel, you will get what is not written here and you will understand quickly. If you feel nothing, you must remember that spirit communes with spirit, not mind. You are functioning on the wrong plane. Relax! Help is on the way.

Reaching Out for Something to Feel

If one is chosen by the Creator to do something, it is within one's power to carry out that assignment even if it is recognized as impossible by nearly everyone else.

Since the key ingredient in the recipe for spiritual power is faith, one's life must be set on a course that produces opportunities for faith to grow. These opportunities for spiritual growth are also opportunities for anxiety and despair. If one's mission is bound to faith in Divine Presence, that mission cannot begin until the spiritual warrior/teacher is rooted and grounded in the unseen.

Those who are set aside for such missions in this world are peculiar people, even among those who are, by definition, peculiar. Only in glancing back along a trail of memories is it somewhat amusing to remember my mother calling me her "peculiar child." Christians are called "peculiar people," so why would she consider me peculiar since she was a Christian?

Asian cultures have a long history of respecting the mystic child, that unique life which comes into the world to illuminate the dark corners of our existence. The records of their deeds and saying are sacred; they are considered a part of the continuous effort of the Living Universe (God) to uplift humanity, soul by soul.

These births are not just recognized in Far Eastern spiritual tradition; the biblical accounts of the prophet Samuel, Moses, the warriors Sampson and Joseph, and the birth of Christ all recognize that help often comes in the body of an innocent child. That child is clueless about his purpose for being until awakened at some point later in life. There is no fixed time or method to that awakening. It is different for everyone.

There are atrocities committed in the world in the name of religion because men assume they know the complete plan of God for those other than themselves. They think they know the mind of God, which is said to be far beyond the ways of man, but they do not understand the nature of their own minds.

The Mystic Child is driven from within. He or she is anchored in emptiness. The intelligence that guides him or her cannot be apprehended by the senses. There is a sense of a presence that need not be proven to the one who perceives it.

Sadguru Sant Keshavadas and I stood outside of New Calvary Baptist Church. The then pastor, Milton A. Reid, a well-known civil rights activist and friend of Dr. Martin Luther King Jr., had permitted the guru to speak in an auditorium adjacent to the sanctuary. Santji had always expressed a desire to reach the black community. "You must bridge the gap between East and West," he said to me. "You must teach black people to harness the power of their minds. There is only so far I can go. You can go further. You can help them understand. Black people are the most spiritual people in the world. If they understood the nature of the mind they could have anything they wanted on the Earth." I received his words quietly. I always accepted what was revealed through Santji as words from my Father. To me, Santji was a manifestation of God the Father, that is, God the Father made himself available to me through the willing vessel of the guru.

From the first moments that I understood the spoken word, I heard that God was the Father. I believed it with the same certainty that I accepted my mother and dad in their roles. There was a moment when I was about 11, a moment when I experienced an epiphany. I approached my dad when he was alone. "Dad, I love you," I said, "but God is my Father." My dad could have said anything, but that was the one moment that he spoke in a sensitive, caring away. He spoke to me in a manner that solidified my faith and cemented him to me and God to him and me, no matter what was to come. My dad looked at me and said without hesitation, "I know. He's my Father, too."

There is a distinct and unmistakable difference between the spirit of a man, the presence of an earthly father, and the presence of the Father Himself. All of my life, I talked to God as my father, as family. I talked to him about my struggles, my defeats, my fears, everything, just as any child would who had complete faith that he had the love and support of his sire. It is because I loved Father for myself, because I longed to serve Him in whatever capacity that He wanted me to, just as Jesus had done, that I could discern Him.

Although I knew there was a being seated before me with a cover story that reflected a life on Earth, I also knew that the dominant spirit in Santji was not Santji. By virtue of the guru's ability to surrender his ego and make himself as nothing, the Spirit of God the Father touched me. In Santji's embrace, I found the comfort and love I had experienced nowhere else. There was no one who saw me as pure soul and loved me as that but Sadguru Sant Keshavadas—that is, no one with a body on the planet. I never cared who was around, small gatherings or large events, given the opportunity, I would rest my head on Santji's knee, and he would rub his fingers through my hair. I was transported to a secret place at those times. No one else was in that world with me, not even he whose arms appeared to embrace me. Santji was the vehicle, not the destination.

Santji's words were spoken to me without instructions. He would give me assignments, but he never told me how to do them. He spoke, I listened. Occasionally, I challenged him. He was always gentle in his responses. I had been on my own for many years. I was a spiritual "samurai." I did not follow anyone blindly nor take anything at face value. I examined everything against the spirit within me. That was my insurance, to try the spirit by the Spirit, to see if it be of God.

Santji told me things. He outlined the need and looked into my eyes. Those dark, yet luminous orbs that were windows gazing on eternity reminded me that I knew exactly what to do. What was in him resonated in me also, cell for cell.

Once when he spoke at a temple in Richmond, Virginia, he called my name and asked me to stand by him. I stood before the gathering of yogis, a mixture of Asian and American devotees. "Kitabu will give the satsang [sermon]," he said.

I walked to the front of the room, joined my palms in a bow to Santji, and turned to speak. When I was finished, Santji stepped forward and said, "The Holy Spirit has spoken." Outside, some Indian devotees followed me about the grounds. "How did you get so close to the Guru?" a woman dressed in a beautiful sari and scarf asked me. "We have the same teacher," I replied. I said no more.

Swimming in One Ocean

Santji said, "The Holy Spirit has spoken." It is an important clue if you want to see into the role and nature of the spiritual teacher. It seems to me that the primary problem with people is that they take some things for granted. The most awesome mistake a human being can make, in my view, is to assume that life, our very existence, is a given. People, routinely, believe that being alive makes sense.

It is a major error to take one's existence and the existence of all things for granted.

I do not hold to the view that the world exists in the way you may experience it. In order to do justice to the subject, I must speak from the place of authority that comes only with direct experience. To waiver, to apologize or bow to views outside of that experience, would render this book of no value.

If truth is universal, as we believe, then the nature of truth will ring familiar. When it is appropriate to quote such a person or persons who bear witness to that universal experience, I will do so, as I have done so far. What is more important is that which springs effortlessly, as this writing comes, from the evolution of my own being, my personal spiritual journey. What was always present with me was also unknown to my mind. My conscious journey was not, at first, a mission to reach out to humanity; it was a relentless quest to spend my life unraveling the mystery of my own being.

There was something calling me, a powerful yearning to return to a home far beyond the cosmos and the understanding that I could do just that. How could I know that if I sank deep within my own being, I would emerge from the journey, not only connected to you, but also to everything and nothing at all? Who would know such a thing? The deeper I went within, the more mystical contacts I had with others along the way who confirmed what was revealed to me in secret. I quickly discovered that "the secret," the mystery of being, was not at all like drinking cool refreshing water while others thirsted in vain. It was more like discovering that every soul swam in the water, like fish swimming in the ocean, but most were unaware that the water was there, or if they believed it, they had yet to give themselves completely to the movement of that water.

What is the gap between East and West? Just how could I, a man born outside of the rich history of Asia, with its tremendous respect for enlightened ones, ever hope to bridge the distance? I lived in a country where the mere darkness of my skin typecast me as powerless. Respect for Dharma (the Teachings) and the emissary of Dharma were necessary to ensure success. There was another problem, one as huge as racism. Just how could one who was born, raised, and steeped in Christianity throughout his life promote in the Bible Belt what sounds an awful lot like Buddhism or Hinduism? How does one do that? I learned early, there was little tolerance in the church for anything not approved or introduced to the body by the preacher.

"They will accept the teaching from you," Santji said.

Fortunately, if you are chosen by God, you are guided by God. You simply do what you are led by the spirit to do. What is not necessary for those who travel by way of the spirit is to formulate an intellectual plan of their own. The chosen do not have to explain or justify their path to themselves or others. That is not to say that we cannot find ourselves embroiled in discussion or debate with some well-read pundit who thinks he knows everything about the Way. He may, in fact, be well-versed in religion and philosophy. He may be able to astound listeners with his knowledge of the ancient writs, but the truth is that such knowledge has no redeeming value where it counts.

Thoughts are objects of perception. They appear in the mind. You are aware of them by the power of the mind itself. The Japanese speak of *nen,* or a thought-instant. The yogis speak of *prakriti* (thought energy). Throughout your life, you have been led to believe that you are educated by what you store in your mind. You are educated by the way you carry yourself in society. Education is not a substitute for wisdom. They are not the same. If you would break free of your carnal prison and realize the truth of your nature, if you would soar among the planets while dining at a state dinner or waiting on customers at 7-Eleven, you can do that and more.

The question is: What are you seeking, information or transformation? If you want information, you are better off setting this book down right now and picking up a scholarly text. If you have a good memory, you will sound like an expert in no time. If you want transformation, it can only be triggered by No-Mind, not by the mind. It is an uncharted course. No-Mind reflects the perfection of the Spirit.

There is something in you that corresponds to the ultimate. Spiritual activity arises out of that reality. The word "emptiness" (*sunyata* in Sanskrit) is often used. It does not indicate nothing, the absence of all things. Before creation, before a single thing existed, there was emptiness. Emptiness is alive with possibility, yet it cannot be classified as a phenomenon or a noumenon. Even though the word "noumenon" refers to that which exists beyond the intellect, such a definition still implies that "something" is out there. To think that there is something that can be grasped becomes another barrier. The word "emptiness" does not apply to God. Any attempt to limit God to a definition is to immediately reduce Him to an object of thought. While God will remain what He is despite that attempt, it is we who lose by trying to categorize Him. I shudder even at my use of the gender word "He." I know that God is not this or that. Sometimes we bow a little to convention, however, or there is no way to communicate.

The only one who can help you find your way through the confusion of this world to the simplicity and power of just being is one who is connected to that truth. It is his nature, just as flying and hunting from the sky is the nature of the eagle. Like you, even the Chosen came as an infant into this world and was exposed to the mind-shaping and soul-imprisoning teachings of the rulers of this realm. Since that person was set aside, however, that is, preordained to his mission before his body was formed in the womb of his mother, the ties that would bind his mind kept falling away. Nothing could cling to it for long.

The Scripture testifies that the god of this world could almost deceive the Elect, the chosen ones of God. Almost is not good enough. Yet it is because those who are sent to help their fellow man are themselves tested to the limit that they are able to help others escape the clutches of deception. So what is the formula, you ask. Just this: What does it take to help you? The question is not asked for your friend or for humanity at large. The question is directed only at you. What does it take to help you? How a teacher approaches you depends entirely on what it will take to break though your misconceptions. Like all spiritual teachers, I am licensed by the Source to employ upaya, skillful means. How will that manifest? Neither you nor I will know. It is lightning striking, thunder rolling, on a bright sunny day. Are you ready? Each step home is a step further into the unknown.

It is written that a Zen master can steal candy from a baby or run off with the farmer's ox.

For 20 years, an old woman supported a Zen monk. She built a hut for him in her backyard and provided food. All he had to do was practice *zazen*, pursue Dharma practice day after day. After so many years had passed, she thought, "I will test this monk and see what he has acquired by way of understanding." Her daughter was beautiful and of the age when she was ripe with desire. She told her daughter, "Go and embrace the monk and say to him, 'What now?'" The young woman did as she was told. She approached the monk and embraced him passionately, then asked, "What now?"

"A withered old tree has no sap," was his immediate reply.

Now by the book, a religionist would probably applaud the monk for his abstinence in the face of temptation. The old woman, however, was incensed.

She told the monk in no uncertain terms, "You did not have to make love to her, but you could have showed compassion for her condition." This monk failed the test.

In the year 1568, the nun Myote entered the quarters of Zen master Kimon to demonstrate her understanding of Zen. She entered his chamber completely naked, but the master was unfazed. As she lay before him, the master pointed his iron *nyo-I,* ceremonial stick, toward her thighs and said, "What trick is this?"

"I present the gate by which all the buddhas of the three realms come into the world," she answered.

"Unless the buddhas of the three realms go in, they cannot come out," the master responded. "Let the gate be entered here and now." So saying he sat astride the nun.

"He who would enter, what buddha is that?" she demanded.

"What is to be from the beginning has no should about it."

The nun retorted, "He who will not give his name is a barbarous brigand who is not allowed to enter."

"Matreiya Buddha who has to be born to save all beings after the death of Shakyamuni Buddha enters the gate."

When the nun made as if to speak, Master Kimon covered her mouth, pointed the nyo-I, and pressed it between her thighs. "Maitreya enters the gate, give birth this instant!"

The nun hesitated.

"This is no true womb. How can it give birth to Maitreya?" he demanded.

The nun cried with great force, "He was born last night." She grabbed the master by the head. "I invite the Buddha to take the top of this head as the lion throne. Let him graciously preach a sermon about it."

"The way is one alone, not two, not three."

"In their abilities, the beings are different in ten thousand ways. How should you stick to one way?" she asked.

The master said, "One general at the head of ten thousand men enter the capital."

(This koan was cited in *Samurai Zen: The Warrior Koans,* by Trevor Leggett.)

The kind of events described in this koan would be considered scandalous in any religious circles, but the purpose of Zen is to free the mind of the individual. It involves the whole being in the process. Myote was a virtuous woman of spotless reputation. When she walked into the room of the master naked, she stripped herself bare of her ego and exposed the womb of the universe. Myote in that moment showed herself in the likeness, the feminine likeness, of the spirit of being. Undivided in mind, there was no one to be ashamed, no one to suppress the flowering of her understanding. Likewise, the master was free in the fullness of the yang expression, all the time pushing against Myote's bold challenge until in her hesitation she demonstrated she was not yet ready to "bear" the Buddha Child. The Son of Man cannot come through a womb that doubts its holiness/wholeness.

In the Zen approach you are *it.* How much freedom do you want? How much can you stand? Show me your freedom now. If you leap without looking back, you will fly. If you turn to glance at the ground, you will crash, screaming. The apostle Paul said, "All things are lawful unto me but all things are not expedient."

How much does the word "all" cover? That which is not expedient suggests the need for voluntary suspension of certain freedoms for the sake of others.

The power of the Zen or awakened mind is unconscious. *Mushin* (No-Mind), *Munen* (No-Thought), and *Muso* (No-Reflection) all point to the nature of that mind. When applied to Bushido (the way of the warrior), the movements of the warrior are not orchestrated by him but come from an untraceable source of wisdom that acts on his behalf. It can be said that Zen activity arises from the place of creation itself.

Empty handed I go
But behold I carry a hoe . . .

The activity of a Zen master does not originate in the realm of thought, so it is nondoing or *wu-wei,* in Chinese. This is like the unhampered movements of an infant. His response to a situation will be determined only by the nature of that situation, not by a conscious guideline. There is a vast difference between those who are trying to become awakened and those who have tamed the bull. The Zen master rides his own spirit, the wind, wherever he chooses to go. What you think of it is of no concern to him. Only if he has agreed to teach, will he cloak himself in ceremonial restraints. You may enter his room looking for a kind word, but if it takes a solid right cross to your chin to reach you, that is what you will get.

If you ask a lofty question, you may be met with deafening silence. Like Forrest Gump's box of chocolates, you never know what you're going to get when you enter the world of Real Zen. Just because one Zen monk was cold like a dead tree, no warmth anywhere, when met by a woman longing for an embrace, does not mean that a master won't scorch her inside and out with Krishna passion. If you draw a sword or gun, I may take it and let you live. The very drawing of your weapon gives me your life, if I want it. Where should this black fire rage? It must go somewhere. As demonstrated through the ages, and underscored by Shakyamuni Buddha, Bodhidharma, Ch'an masters of China, Zen masters of Japan, and others, the insight garnered through the enlightenment experience is user-specific. It functions in the cultural context of the vehicle. How would a Tathagatha of African ancestry express his Zen? He would naturally embody the passion of the ancestors. Would he scorch the earth to avenge their blood at the hands of a self-serving enemy or would forgiveness be offered and the awesome power inherent in his being be redirected elsewhere? Legend says that Krishna made war against demons. What a terrifying mission. When he was on furlough, he could always be found among the pretty young maidens, playing music, dancing, sometimes creating a scheme to see them naked. The demon fighters need plenty of fun and much love because they must always return to face what others run from. What will Tathagatha do? What business is it of yours? The truth is no one knows, not even Tathagathas.

No flesh and blood crosses this threshold and keeps its life. If you are not sure of what you are, keep to your thoughts and stand back. A master may embrace you or cut you down. Here is the realm of Dharma, not the haven of ordinary men. You are responsible for your own choice. It is not a game. Here in this realm, you must stand on your own faith or fall. The heaven of the masters is terrestrial. It is right before them.

Has it ever been a secret that spirit-centered beings could move freely on the same Earth as ordinary men?

> And the sons of God came to earth and found the daughters of men comely and married among them, any of them they chose . . . From this number came the heroes and men of mighty repute. (Gen. 6)

If you would enter the bed of a son or daughter of God, you must divest yourself of all your clothing, most of all, the garment you call your body. From the stories that are told, many have entered the bedchamber of the masters as a spiritual consort and left as flesh and blood. Flesh cannot enter the gate. It can only be picked up on the way back and down.

From the carnal state, everything is as it appears. There are many dimensions the eyes cannot see that are open only to souls as they soar back homeward.

If you would be transformed, you must read a book with no pages, written by a writer without words; but even that is not good enough. You must go even further. You must explore this pageless and wordless book, giving up any quest for knowledge, thus approaching it with no thought.

You have learned to fill your mind with information. This is the age of information, after all. If information is the mark of enlightenment, why do we still lack peace on earth and good will toward men? Why do we still seek new and more efficient ways of self-destruction? It is said that knowledge is power, and so it is. Knowledge helps you succeed in the dominion of the known. That which can be grasped and catalogued by the mind locks the mind to the realm of cause and effect, flesh and the Devil. By flesh and the Devil is meant the dominion of impermanence and mind over spirit.

XVII

Read without Words: The First Nen

If people call you weird, peculiar, or crazy long enough, it is natural to seek to understand why. It becomes obvious that they are comparing your actions and reactions to various incidents and situations according to what is deemed to be the norm. When my spiritual teacher, Sadguru Sant Keshavadas, was a little boy, he was taken to a temple where he had an experience of God as Light *(Panduranga).* The young boy was so overcome with love and devotion for God that he fell upon the ground reciting the name of God over and over. His parents were taken aback by this behavior and very much concerned because no one could arouse him from his state of *samadhi* (concentration). Eventually, the family learned from the village priest that their son was not crazy, but that he was blessed of God. He was destined to serve God as guru. From that time on, people looked at him differently. He soon gained the blessing of the village; after all, it was a good thing to have a living guru in your midst.

Even in India, the home of countless mystics, peculiar behavior is not automatically attributed to divine visions or presence. In America, such occurrences are not even factored into the national consciousness. In America, spiritual experiences are seen to be synonymous with religion. They are relegated to a designated building and time. There are boundaries of time and space, form and protocol. God is not free in America.

He must stay in His assigned place. Those who worship Him, most of them good citizens, remain obedient to the powers of this world. It is a virtue to recognize God and His virtues on Sunday. It is suspect to speak of His majesty on Monday or the rest of the week. It is a good thing to applaud the actions of body and mind all week long, but few dare speak above a whisper about the doings of Spirit.

In the Bible Belt of the South, in this case, Virginia, there are churches to be found everywhere. They are only blocks apart. They come in all styles and sizes, from the huge auditoriums with chandeliers to the tiny storefronts. They also come in cultural styles. When I was a child, the same Jesus Christ reached out from the cross to save souls in the distant future, but his servants had to have matching skin color. No black skin was welcome in a church set aside for whites. It was not true in the reverse. Whether it was because blacks were powerless to make rules whites obeyed or because they were more gracious, whites could enter and worship in any black church without incident. This seldom happened, however, the noted exception being when white politicians came to woo the black vote as more and more blacks registered at the polls.

Spiritual garb, the ritual dress for black churchgoers, was suits and ties for the men and dresses for the women. Their hair would be neatly hot-combed and greased. Anyone not dressed in Sunday clothes and on their way to a church on Sunday were tagged as heathens.

From the earliest moment of my life in this body, I observed in silence all that was going on around me.

Perhaps because of this profound silence, this samadhi of hearing, I could sense the more subtle vibrations in time and was captivated to the point of ecstasy by the power of music, no matter what kind of music played. Each genre took me to a different dimension.

Being drawn into this silence, I am aware now that I did not experience a boundary. There was no location. In the early hours of the morning when my mother checked on her children and found my eyes open night after night, she was always fascinated and incredulous at the same time. According to her, as early as three years old, I seemed to have no need of sleep. She called me "Doll Baby Eyes."

"What are you looking at, baby?" she would ask.

The truth is that I was just looking, in the same manner that I listened. I just looked, I just listened. I was looking at nothing, listening to nothing. I saw and heard only what arose in the environment.

I continued in this way through the early years. Listening to my brother and sisters talk about me now, I recognize that they saw me as an outside observer in the family. It was not that I never participated in the family circle, but more often I was in my own place.

Only in retrospect, after having walked with those who have approached the inner path from many different schools—Taoists, Zen masters, gurus, Christian and Islamic mystics—have I reached the vantage point to distill the peculiar from the norm.

Only now can I see the evidence of the path I was given. It was always right there. It is that experience that will help you.

The stories of Asian masters are marvelous and inspiring, but it is also true that their path is not accessible to most people born in the West. People, even the enlightened ones, speak from the experience of their own backgrounds and language. Santji understood. What was needed, what is needed, are those who embrace the secrets of the East, not through scholarship, but by receiving the Light of Asia, Mind to mind, without losing the uniqueness and integrity of their own identities. These people know for themselves that fire is hot and water is wet. They know because they are not intruders. They are each a key to the house. Each is a rightful heir.

Rude Awakening

As a young child, I drank in life naturally, without blocking. Like all children, I chased grasshoppers, climbed trees, and enjoyed the sounds of birds and crickets; but there was something more going on.

I was six years old when the silence of my sleep was broken by shouting. What happened that night may have been the pivot upon which my life was to turn for decades to come. I woke up in the middle of the night disturbed by a sound from the hallway. My brother Raymond lay sleeping next to me. He was younger. I leaned off the side of the bed and saw my mother and father in the hall. Harsh words were being spoken. I could feel vibrations of anger and fear. I listened. My mother screamed something and I saw my father's hand rise in the air above her face. In that instant, I glanced about the room and saw a jar of Royal Crown Hair Pomade on the dresser in front of me. I leapt out of bed and ran to get it. As soon as it was in my hand, I stepped from the darkness of my room into the light from the door and hurled the jar with all my might. I watched it tumble in the air. In that moment, I knew it would hit Dad in the face. I wanted to call it back, but I couldn't. I watched as the jar moved in slow motion, guided unerringly like a missile fired from a submarine, like a stone shot out of David's sling. The jar connected with a sharp report and he grabbed his face, forgetting my mother. My heart throbbed. I wanted to protect my mother, but I did not want to hurt my father. For a second, I froze, then realizing, believing that I had done something very wrong, I dove to the floor and slid under the bed.

Recovering from the shock, my father looked for his assailant. Raymond was still sleep. Suddenly, the entire queen-size bed was lifted from one side. A hand grabbed my ankle and held me in the air, my head dangled toward the floor.

"Don't!" my mother yelled. "He was just defending his mother."

My father didn't listen. He pulled off his belt and beat my buttocks and legs while he held me in that position. The physical whipping was not administered to kill me. Whatever it did was not as painful as what I felt seeing the jar thrown by my hand hit his face. How could I convey to him that I loved him anyway? How could I explain that I did not consciously set out to hurt him? It happened. I was driven to protect my mother, compelled by a cry for help. I forgot myself. She was the center of the universe, the reason I had breath. It was all I felt at that moment until the impact. Then all I could feel was the pain of my father.

Usually, after midnight, the world is quiet except for the normal night sounds. In the suburbs where we used to live, the night music was provided by crickets. Passing cars were rare. As I sat up in bed, seeing nothing but the void that is the room without light, my body just received the sounds and the movements of the air. I had neither thoughts about it nor any feeling that I was doing anything special. I did not know why I sat up night after night listening to nothing or why it soothed me. All I know was that there was comfort in the void where nothing moved.

Knowing nothing about other cultures at that early age, I assigned no name to my behavior. It was not a practice. This way was natural to me.

What I know now, in retrospect, was that this sitting in stillness, the tuning in to nothing in particular must have sharpened my senses in a peculiar way. I could feel the pain and emotions of others with great intensity.

If a person was sad, even a stranger, I felt it within me. If they were pleased, annoyed, happy, it did not matter; I felt their experience as my own. The partition provided by flesh and blood did not keep me out. In feeling what others felt, there was a need to share with them. I needed to help them carry their burden or celebrate the moments of joy as my own.

This capacity to empathize in the extreme was not something of which I was conscious. Later, as I got older, other people, including family members, would make me aware of it. Often their comments were given as criticism. "You make me sick the way you're always defending other people. You don't know them. Why do you take their side?" If a person was wounded, the underdog, I naturally stood by them. It was a trait tailor-made to provide a life of trouble. Whatever compelled me to take such a stance was not weakened by fear of consequences, and there were consequences.

A Transmission from Jesus

"My yoke is easy," Jesus said. "My burden is light." I became intimately acquainted with Jesus early in life. My communion with him was so deep and personal that a lifetime of learning and unlearning and exposure to many avenues of thought never dented my faith in him one iota. It is important to the exploration of soul that I share the story of our encounter with you. It may help you to understand Jesus Christ in a different way than the traditional party line. It may help you understand yourself.

It is important that we approach the subject of the true self, that we enter the gate of the temple, with *shoshin*, or "beginner's mind," as Shunryu Suzuki Roshi liked to say. You must leave your preconceived ideas, prejudices, and dogmas on the floor outside with your shoes. What is true will always be true. If it is not so, why would you willfully cling to a known lie? You cannot know yourself though concepts. Seekers of truth will find truth.

Although, obviously, my parents were not perfect, they consciously allied themselves with God. They prayed, read the Bible daily, groomed the children on the Scriptures, and did everything they could to instill a sense of awe and respect in us for the creator of the world. In this, they did a great job. It is because they began such grounding early in our lives that there was never a question among my siblings about the existence of God. There is an inherent conflict between the way man's mind functions and the Spirit. Thus the Scripture warns that, "There is enmity between the mind and the Spirit." It is because of that rift that people who would act from love and peace can go in the opposite direction without notice. It depends on what nature is in charge of the body at that moment: the mind or the spirit.

One Sunday morning, I was in the balcony at Zion Bethel Church chatting with my friends during the sermon, as we always did. I was nine. My brother Raymond, who was eight, was also with us. For some reason, I stopped talking and began to listen intensely to Reverend Joseph Copeland talking about the mission of Jesus Christ. He spoke of the Atonement.

As I listened, the church and the whole of the congregation, Raymond and my friends, all faded from view. Even though this was happening, I had no fear. There was a thick black cloud blocking my vision, but it cleared enough for me to see a figure in the distance. There, stretched out and bleeding, was Jesus Christ. His head was hanging down, but as I gazed upon him, he looked up into my eyes. I knew that he saw me and I also knew that he was aware that I was looking at him from the future, just as I knew I was seeing him through a live connection to the past.

He continued to look into my eyes until I felt a flooding taking place. I was suddenly overcome with great sorrow. I felt wretched and unclean. We shared the experience for a while, but Jesus never spoke to me. He did not have to. I understood. The message had been sent. Everything was suddenly back to normal and the pastor was concluding his sermon. One thing had changed. I was no longer an innocent nine-year-old. I was weighed down by a burden so great I could barely keep from crying.

When Pastor Copeland stood before the church and gave the invitation to sinners, I got up immediately. I felt like the most horrible sinner who ever lived. I focused, hearing the chorus of "amens" spoken by the faithful at seeing a child walk down the aisle. Pastor Copeland held out his arms as I approached him, but as I entered those huge wings of his black garment something shifted. It was not the spirit of Pastor Copeland I felt at all, but the spirit of Jesus Christ embracing me through the vehicle of the pastor's body. The weight fell from me and I felt light and airy.

We had connected soul to soul, but then, in only moments, Jesus demonstrated what is possible when we reach beyond the realm of cause and fact and the known laws. We also connected in the physical realm.

When the student is ready, the master will appear. When I trace the roots of my spiritual journey, I recognize that my parents provided my primary conscious foundation but that Jesus himself was the initiating master. The goal of a master is to raise up those like himself, masters. While religions are a repository of teachings, masters are not of a religion. Earlier, I wrote that one could only be initiated by a living master. At the time I had this experience with Christ, he and I both were in our bodies but in separate dimensions of time. The link with his mind was direct and alive. Though such a phenomenon can be explained, explaining it would defeat our purpose. It is enough for me that it occurred. That may not be enough for you. You would be making the common mistake of trying to analyze a spiritual event with your intellect. Engage your spirit instead.

Learn to Accept the Mystery

Mastery is not something you have over someone else or even something to cling to after you attain it. If you reach that point of transformation, you will find yourself in a peculiar place. You must drop your attachment to the tool that got you there in order to exercise the freedom you've achieved. In Zen, it is said that Zen is a stone that is used to knock on a door. It is thrown away when the door is open. There are many people who worship their religions even more than God. Somewhere, a vital message has been left out. Spiritual teachings are about renewal, transformation, and restoration of the *Jivatma* (individual soul) to its rightful place in the scheme of all things. Jesus is clear:

> The wind bloweth where it listeth, and thou hearest the sound thereof, but canst not tell whence it cometh, and whither it goeth: so is every one that is born of the Spirit. (John 3:8)

Be honest. If you are currently locked into a formal institutional approach to God, does this verse describe you? If you fancy yourself a philosopher, an agnostic, whatever you label yourself, do you know the freedom and spontaneity suggested by this verse? If you do not, you will never know it playing by the rules of men, even if those men are standing on the highest of pulpits. You must meet the master face to face. You must touch him.

I have heard people sing the hymn so many times in church, "He touched me . . ." I know the worshippers are speaking of that spiritual touch that opens the heart. I wonder sometimes how many people know the Master can touch them, embrace them, share a cup of tea or coffee with them, if they desire it. There are laws and there are higher laws. Would you like to have tea with the Master? It is not hard at all when you communicate soul to soul.

Several years ago, my heart was heavy. I felt that no one understood my mission, not even my family. As I walked down Monticello Street in Norfolk, Virginia, an old black man with a cane called out to me. "Come here, son. Don't worry. People may not understand you now, but in two or three hundred years your message will be clear," he said. I gazed into his eyes as I did Santji's. Santji was now fully on the other shore. I recognized the same spirit. "Buy me a cup of coffee," he said. I sat with him, listening and sipping coffee. Then, as he commanded, I drove him home, never to see him again or to remember where I went.

When I walked out of church the Sunday of my encounter with Jesus, the world was different. The sun was brighter, the air was sweet and fresh, and the people who milled about the church in their colorful clothes seemed invisible, in a sense. I saw them, but they were more like illusions of people. Inside, I felt my being burning with love for all beings. The fire was so hot in me that I could barely finish dinner before I was outside walking down the street, talking about the Lord to whomever would listen. It seemed to me that everyone would want to experience what I was feeling. What I discovered was that there was a barrier that was hard to penetrate. They could hear my words, but they did not receive my communication. Mind was in conflict with spirit. I was saddened that I could not communicate my joy.

Until my mystical meeting with Christ, I had never encountered another soul in the void. It is significant that while I was under the age of puberty and still playing with toys, I learned that time, distance, space, even people were separated by the flimsiest of veils. The Jesus I met was still alive in his suffering, so his body was very much in the realm of cause and effect. Time was not a barrier to a living connection between us. The bridge was spirit.

Unbeknownst to me, the young Santji was learning about his own spiritual heritage. He who had been awestruck by a *darshan* (vision) of Panduranga, God as Light, was surrendering to his own Inner Guru.

Though it was not something we ever discussed, I now see the correlation, Santji embraced God as Light and I had a darshan of Jesus Christ, called the Light of the World. The Supreme Lord leaves nothing to chance.

I was nine years old, but still heaven charged me with a mission that would not wait for me to mature. The force of the Light striking from without, combined with the silently illuminating spirit which was with me from the beginning, split me apart from those around me. Even though it happened, I did not understand the alienation. As the Father God says in the Torah, "I Am That I Am." Man is in the habit of fishing for explanations that do not exist, then making up something to fill the void when he comes up empty.

Kate Turner's peculiar child became more peculiar with time in the eyes of others. There is no reason to question what happens within oneself when it arises naturally and unsought. How do we know that others don't have the same experiences?

We are schooled to grasp for facts and the provable. It is no wonder that faith is hard to come by after we reach our teens. By faith, I do not mean mere belief. Faith to me is the ability to stand on absolutely nothing with the comfort of resting on solid ground.

Sitting in the dark listening to the stillness for hours on end as a child caused me to be rooted in a living reality that I had no need to see. What fascinated me was what I could see. The world before my eyes seemed teeming with mystery. The most intriguing meditation I had was how it could exist at all. I did not accept that the visible world was the ground, the foundation for all else. The sense of mystery did not ever leave me.

Transformation

So we come back to the question. Transformation does not come from knowing who you are. "Who" is fleeting, arbitrary. The question you must answer by direct experience remains, what is man? What are you? There are many things we do that involve pleasing other people, but to embark on this quest is not one of them. This is a mission you must undertake for yourself. Only your faithful and sincere reaching will win the support necessary to guide you to that sacred temple where the blessing of realization is bestowed. If you can sense the urgency and unequalled excellence of this pursuit, realization will become the primary focus of your life. So awesome is the moment of awakening that those who have attained it say that to have it at the final moment of your life is sufficient.

Do you want to help the world? The mind gives us grand delusions about our effect in making changes. What is wrought by the mind, like memory, fades in time. Real change takes place at the spiritual level.

Who knows what needs to be done? The spiritual teacher must first become the spiritual student. He who masters his mind must surrender it.

"Not my will but thy will be done."

So those who would help you break free of the trap, those who are born free of the illusion, must be imprisoned in the deepest dungeon of human despair so that they will feel and know, suffer and struggle until the day that the wings they were born with come alive on their own and beat down the walls of illusions with a sound like thunder, and they catapult back into the vastness of unlimited life.

If you would help mankind, do not stand above; stand below and push. Do not be first; be the last.

If you have suffered, you have survived for a reason. Your suffering is a seed that will give rise to a beautiful flower when properly cultivated.

Seeing that I am quick to smile and easy to laugh, one man said that he wished he had my life.

"You have never suffered a day," he said.

"If you had my life, you would have killed yourself the first week," I said. He could not even begin to imagine the depths of my suffering, and I doubt I will ever attempt to convey more than a taste to anyone. God knows. That is sufficient.

Intentional Spiritual Protocol

It is for theologians and philosophers to engage in debates about the existence and will of God. Those who are preordained to the service of the spirit have no religion to promote. This does not mean that they do not participate in the religion of their family nor decry the names of God, such as they are taught. For those who are ever-linked to the Originator of all things, the names are like adding another grain of sand to the beach. When they are among worshippers, they follow the spirit of their intent. Thus, the spiritual votary is not concerned with name or formality. In Him, there is only *That.* To reference that presence, even as the One, is saying too much.

As the tree gives shade where it stands, so also does the teacher/master. A tree may be planted in a field owned by a farmer, but it will give shade to anyone who comes to sit beneath it. The farmer may feel he owns the tree, but the tree has no mind to be possessed. It withholds its fruit from no one; the farmer, the guests, even the thief is welcome. This is the Mind of a master, the Mind known not only by Christ, but also by all the Buddhas and all the masters who ever walked the earth and ever will. Like the tree, that Mind withholds its fruit from no one. It is not a mind that can be possessed; no one can hold it to themselves so that it is exclusive to them or to their sect.

In Shakyamuni, it was Buddha Mind. Five hundred and twenty-six years later, it is the mind that is in Christ, the Son of God. In the Kamakura District of Japan, it became the mind of the samurai, and a new type of warrior was born. This same Mind produced great warriors who were the antithesis of the samurai, the Shaolin monks. The seed of Bodhi (the awakened mind) produced a genius that affected all aspects of life.

If you don't sign up, you don't receive the benefits. Your mind is like your laptop. You have the password to enter Windows, but you also need an ISP (Internet service provider) to go online. If you know nothing about the Internet, have never heard of its capabilities, you are handicapped. Once you learn that it is out there, you must choose to connect. Of course, there is more than one provider, so be careful. Know what you're seeking.

You can remain offline and unto yourself, content to muse in word processing software or to play games. This does not mean you're safe, however. Your laptop was configured before you were even aware of its existence, so even your thoughts are programs written by an unknown source.

You can join a local network, but then you will have friends along the highway of delusion. You are all connected to a single CPU (central processing unit). Controlled by the system. You are guaranteed to receive data designed to keep you locked in that tiny universe. "The Matrix" will have you secured.

If you become intuitively aware or believe in the message of one who has realized the truth, you will understand that you are viewing the world through programs designed to deceive you about what you are, designed to hide your potential from you.

If you come to feel the truth of that, you can reach out in an exhaustive search. You can seek an ISP that matches the needs of your heart. Once online, there is no end to the network. This is the *sangha,* the living network of the Universal Mind, in shorthand, the Zen mind, your true mind.

There is great conflict in the world around us, wars of hate and greed, disharmony and alienation, because the outer world reflects what is within us. While knowledgeable men may consider the spiritual teachings of all cultures superstitions, the chosen ones pick up the books and recognize a higher science that reveals the secrets of the universe to them. For many years, I found it dangerous to share my thoughts with others. Once, when I was walking through Times Square in New York with a new acquaintance, I unveiled my vision of the universe to him. Before I could get to the best part, he started to scream and ran down the street. I was horrified, but I realized what I had done and ran after him. When I caught up with him, I brought the vibration down. I talked of mundane things with the same intensity as I had spoken of my other understanding and he returned to normal. Despite the warning, however, I did not really understand what was happening. Though I had been initiated by Zen master Nomura Roshi, I had yet to meet the guru who would work with and refine my understanding. I was dangerous then, not only to others, but also to myself.

Years later, when I enjoyed the privilege of sitting privately at the feet of my guru whenever the need arose, he reminded me again that the swan was the symbol of the guru because the mystical swan could sip milk mixed with water, extract the milk, and leave the water. The illustration bears repeating because it shows how the guru or spiritual teacher differs from the average reader of Scriptures. It signifies that we were given the ability to discern the true meaning of Scriptures of all cultures. Immediately, I remembered the words of the Bible, "Study to show yourself approved, a workman that needeth not to be ashamed, rightly divining the word of truth." I understood that the verse was telling the believer that the meaning was not obvious but hidden.

The student of the Way, the disciple, is charged to probe deeply to find the treasure hidden in the words. Unfortunately, it has become common for people to delight in just memorizing and quoting Scriptures, sometimes to bolster their own position. Scriptures are means to work on oneself. When I shared my insight with my New York acquaintance, I took him to a place he had not chosen to go. He was not ready. This is a path that honors free will. The diamond of realization cannot be attained by force, not by the force of your will nor by force of the Divine. It is said, "Behold! I stand at the door and knock. If any man should open the door, we will come in and sup with him."

If, by your free will, you choose to open the door to the Master (the Lord), they will both enter. In William Holman Hunt's famous painting, *The Light of the World,* there is no handle on the side where the Master Jesus is. It is important to point out that only Jesus is at the door, so who is this "we" he is talking about?

Hint: The Incarnate Lord is the host of the one you cannot see. You cannot move the palm of your hand without moving the back of your hand at the same time.

Preordained or not, we must choose to open the door to the Lord as a matter of course. Santji did the same thing when he received God as

Light. Jesus did it when he agreed to be baptized, even though he was already a master by our standards. We all have a choice to make. Man has two hands, a left and a right. If you know what the right hand is doing, you will not know what the left is doing. If you know what the left hand is doing, you will not be able to follow the movements of the right. There must be one side left to the unconscious, to faith, to the spirit.

In my case, I was rooted deeply in the unknown. I was at home and comfortable with the void. I had to reach out to the manifest Lord, the Incarnate Teacher. Those who are grounded in the incarnate aspect of the Godhead must learn to reach into the void to connect to the preincarnate Lord to enter the hidden dimensions of faith. If you come to this moment with a pragmatic mind, you will seek facts and proof that such exists. As long as you work in this manner, you will fail to penetrate the mystery. You must learn to accept that there are Higher Laws that work beyond your comprehension. You do not need to know how they work; they just do. If you put them to the test, you will discover soon enough there is something working behind the scenes. This is Dharma.

It is a safe assumption that all human beings need food and water, clothing and shelter to survive. We may say this is a simple law of existence. While this example may be easy to understand because it is an observable fact, Dharma may not be so simple to understand. For all that you see that contributes to the life of mankind, there is far more at work that is unseen. When harmony is lost, there must be a way to restore equilibrium. For mankind, the loss of harmony occurred when we lost connection with the true nature of our being or Original Mind. For countless centuries, we functioned far below our potential. We exercise a mind that sees through a distorted window. Dharma is the path that leads to restoring that nature, the law that, when practiced, heals that which was broken.

Faith in Dharma triggers the mind of a true student of the Way. A true student of Dharma is a disciple of the Unknown. The Unknown is the teacher within the teacher, the master behind the master. He is called many names, but has no personal name. He is the Word, the Audible Sound Current, Shabh, the JagadGuru, the World Teacher. His word is the immovable mountain, the foundation upon which all spiritual masters stand. This is the reason that once teachers enter into that secret refuge where the Holy Spirit resides, they speak with one accord. Those who function as the spiritual master, the teacher, do so because they yield their minds. Spirit is the master of the master, not the mind.

In the biblical account of the fall of man, the serpent injected a seed of doubt in Adam about his perfection. That was all it took to engineer his fall.

Adam was mind personified, thus he had no mind. The moment he turned his ability on himself, he became divided between being and believing in a mind to search. Adam or Man became a figment of his own imagination, his own mind. This state of affairs superimposed an imaginary man on top of Original Man. The function of Mind/Man was to operate within the dominion of Earth that was its dominion. Tricked by the serpent, man lost his proper focus.

The Original Man did not have a religion, nor did he need one. He had an ongoing relationship with the spiritual being as Father. Nothing more was needed.

What we have is a conflict between our own mind and spirit that affects our contact with others in the world and our equilibrium. The ego is a Nine-Headed Dragon that devours the truth and resists taming with all of its might. Like the mythological creature of that name, it grows a new head every time you cut one off.

When we believe that we are a "who," someone special or someone who is not important, it serves to block us from expanding to recognize our true nature.

Not only is it impossible to label that nature in the category of this or that or any other category, it is impossible to assess with the mind. It is important that that point be stressed again and again.

Thus you must decide. If you are going to pride yourself on knowing, accumulating, and cataloguing information, this is definitely not your path.

We will approach the path in two ways, but both approaches require that you leave something at the door with your shoes. Remember where you are entering. There is no one here to impress with your learning. This is a place of unlearning.

Forgive the pun, but it is clear now why we need to be cross-trained as spiritual teachers. We must be prepared to meet the needs of the time and place we are assigned to. We will probe this matter of soul further in the supernatural sense as relating to God and eternity and then we will look at soul in your everyday life, the true focus of Zen.

To those of you who, like me, grew up in a Christian church, there is nothing here to fear. Nothing is said that has not been pointed to in the Scriptures. The term "guru" is not specific to any religion. A guru is one who is ordained to dispel the darkness of the mind. As such, he or she can and is born into all cultures and all religions, although the title by which this person is known may differ. Genuine gurus are of the order of Melchizedek, because, as mentioned earlier, they are unborn, without beginning or end, as far as their consciousness goes. The human experiences connect with the infinite, so the guru sits in the stream between worlds. In this position, he is one with both man and God, but functions as a servant, not a Lord, to humanity.

No one need fear the teachings of a guru because the guru has no agenda of his own. The moon illuminates the darkness. Some people admire the moon; others shut it out with blinds. The moon radiates light because its nature is to do so. The guru being guru is not a choice. Those who are drawn to him receive according to their capacity; those who are not are free to go their way. People of all religions and none at all find their way to the feet of the guru. They don't understand. If you find the feet of the guru, you don't need to declare your religion; The Lord already knows you.

If you receive the ambassador, you accept his Lord.

XVIII

The Light Shines in the Darkness: The Transmission of the Lamp

The symbol that follows represents how God reaches out to everyone. His guru, symbolized by the swan, floats on the ocean of God, accessible to all who seek him, regardless of their religion. By the power of the Holy Spirit, the guru acts under the direct authority of the Supreme Identity, the Fatherhood of God. He communes with the soul of man, not the mind of man.

There is more than one type of cellular phone. Each phone has its own number. Although there are various telephone companies, the technology that makes cellular phones possible is the same for all of them. Men also come in types, and there are diverse roles we play in life. It is important to be clear about yours, to have faith in your own ability and mission.

We must enter this path by faith. There is no substitute and no other key that will open the doors of the mystery to you. To be born a spiritual teacher means that you recognize the Scriptures, all Scriptures as the science of God. We act on them as truth. The truth of the phenomenal world is founded on a different principle. It is much like the laws of gravity. They are true on the planet and in the nonexistence outside Earth's atmosphere.

We know that Original Man was not born. He did not come to be through nine months of gestation in the womb of a woman. He was created. That means he came from nothing, from nowhere, into a world of colors, sound, and multiple sensations. The first man spoken of in the Scriptures had nothing within him to assess, not a single image or thought. There was no past life, no ancestors, no genetic antecedents to direct his behavior. Every act of this man was *munen muso,* without thought or reflection. His movements were naturally fluid and effortless because there was only his will at work. This man was whole (holy). His being was as seamless as the robe of Jesus.

The first man knew nothing of a God. There was no faculty in him to question his existence. That meant God had to introduce Himself to that man by "appearing to him." This established communication between different polarities. The Bible says that the Father appeared to Adam in a form. He walked on the Earth. So began the precedence for God the Father communing with man in a body that looks like his own.

The fallen man was damaged. Now he saw something within himself, something that could not possibly be there for real, since he was the same man who was created out of nothing. Nevertheless, this flaw in consciousness produced another type of man, a mental being, a creature driven by the mind.

How do you rescue man from his delusion?

You send a brother man to him to teach him about the error. When this fails, you send a brother who possesses the means to restore the broken mind. But even this is not enough, so you send a brother who reflects the Original Mind and the Creating Spirit to stand before them seamlessly unifying the whole in one. But even this is not enough. Though the hookup is complete, the prototype is still waiting for the signal that shows the message has been received. How is the Master to know that man got the message?

"I and the Father are one. I would ye be one as we are one."

A guru is able to discern the jewel hidden in the shell of Scripture. While studying the spiritual teachings of many cultures, I did not discover anything that diminished the magnificence of what I learned under the banner of Christianity. In fact, I only found confirmation of the teachings of the Holy Spirit, everywhere, as well as proof that disciples of all masters had the ability to cloud the clarity of the teachers with their opinions and uncanny knack for taking that which was meant to uplift all mankind and making it exclusive to their own group.

Jesus said, "I am the way, the truth and life, no man cometh unto the Father but by me."

As a Christian first, I know that what I am about to say would create loads of trouble for me if I spoke it from a pulpit. Krishna said, "I am the me in everyone." If we set aside the name for a moment and consider the "what," Krishna is represented as an incarnation of the Supreme Godhead. Now, personally, I fully expect that the Supreme Godhead can incarnate anytime, anyplace, and under any name He chooses. It is not my call. What I must be able to do, however, is to know who is speaking. I must recognize Him. "My sheep always know my voice," the Holy Spirit as Jesus says.

There is only One Voice of the Godhead. That voice, that wisdom, is the Holy Spirit.

The statement sounds just like the Holy Spirit speaking. No matter who the Holy Spirit speaks through, the statement is unequivocally bold. This is so . . . period.

Long ago, when I realized that I was being spiritually taught, I realized that I was also being tested. God gives pop quizzes. How will you learn the difference between what is mental and what is spiritual if you are not exposed to both? How you respond to a test is the vital lesson.

There is no comparison between a mental reaction and a spiritual one. When you have tasted that distinctive flavor for yourself, nothing else will ever suffice.

You can say anything you want. You can think any way you want. You may fool others, but it will be meaningless where it counts. You cannot enter the higher region by mental action. Your soul will never be freed by your intellect. There is a way to undo the damage done so long ago. It is like a child verbally abused by a parent. He grows up to think himself inadequate. Only a series of thoughts separate him from excellence, but if he never probes to discover the source of his problem, he is doomed to live a diminished life.

The way is ancient, but the modern guru and Zen masters are not married to ancient ways. Direct experience means you address the world you live in now in the language of ordinary men. You see clearly.

The preferred relationship of God with man is personal, not institutional. It is how the Scriptures speak not only of His relationship to the first man, but also to others who remembered Him. This kind of relationship can only happen when you realize that it is proper and desired. Thus in Jeremiah, God says, "If ye seek me with all your heart, ye shall surely find me." In addition to this promise, the Scriptures indicate that God is capable of having friends and unique love relationships with individuals. Thus it is said that King David was a man after God's own heart. Keep in mind that, in addition to being a faithful warrior and lover of God, David desired a woman, Bathsheba, enough to commit adultery and then engineer the death of her husband, Uriah, so that he could marry her. Of course, God saw all of that, and still he loved him. What a friendship!

God forgives. Humans are another story altogether.

If you're accustomed to seeing God as some distant possibility, you have pushed Him to that extreme place in your mind. The handle to the door of you is on your side, remember. If you open that door with an inviting heart, something marvelous will happen.

First, you must know that what you are is a reflection of what God is, just as a tiny drop of ocean water is akin to the whole of the ocean.

You came out of the ocean. The ocean is calling you. It is really that simple. A guru cannot fathom unbelief in God. Perhaps that is because the guru never forgets that the ocean is all around him. If the drop, or guru, becomes self-possessed for a period of time, he switches his concentration to a private channel, so to speak. There he may have no conscious contact with God for as long as necessary to enjoy fully his role as a single human entity, but even then the presence of God is felt. Sometimes God ebbs and man flows. Other times, man ebbs and God flows.

In a worship service, people focus on the presence of God through the means of Scripture reading, singing, and listening to a sermon. These are effective tools for evoking the Spirit of God and raising the level of vibrations around us. When we worship in a group, we tend to praise an external God, one to be found high above the sun, the moon, and the stars; yet this is not the God, the person of the Trinity preached by Jesus Christ. For Jesus, his Father, his God, was present in the desert, by the well, on the water, yet not to be worshiped in the mountains or the hills. Jesus hinted at a God who lived in a most special place: "When you have seen me, you have seen the Father." He made himself the example of the message, "The Kingdom of heaven is within you." Some texts add, "and among you." Jesus shot the message deep. Unfortunately, the masses could not get it. God prefers to live in the luxuriously appointed mansion He created for the purpose, your soul.

It is because we are like God that we can block His entrance with our will. You must ask Him to enter. When He enters the secret place within you, you will begin to feel the refreshing breeze that is soul-shuddering as it starts to awaken. You can only know the spirit by the Spirit. Your spirit will learn how to function as such when the Spirit is alive in you. The guru sitting before you is the manifestation of that which is within. Thus the guru is the first to tell you that what comes is not from him but through him. He is the instrument, not the musician.

If you wait until you enter a church to acknowledge God, you will have taught your mind to associate only that place or circumstance with God. You will not experience Him when you step back outside and get in your car. You are practicing to leave Him behind. Remember the drop of water in the ocean. The drop is in the ocean, but the ocean is also one with the drop. They cannot be separated. The path of the prodigal son or daughter only admits one person. What you have is your Father, the Creator of your being, reaching out to bring you home in Him. This is not religion. This is the reason for religion. Somehow the personal aspect of the story gets lost amid the pomp and circumstance. When you sit at the feet of the guru, your approach is different. Instead of waiting for God to call you home, you invite Him to come live with you, in you.

Examine this possibility from a religious viewpoint and you may worry that having God around would really cramp your style; but God has no religion. Religion is mankind's approach to God, not God's approach to mankind. God was looking for someone to talk to, someone witty and unpredictable, and someone who, though gifted on his own, would still need someone along the way. It is nice to be needed, after all. God was looking for some friends and, as humans will do, we let Him down.

You cannot be accessible to God by being formal. If you're inclined to see God in this way, you may miss Him as he sits in the Laundromat, hoping you'll notice Him and come chat. We see things and people all the time, but we can only cross over into the spiritual realm when we ourselves are living spirits. It takes one to know one.

When you make the transition to predominantly spirit instead of predominantly mind, you will be able to traverse the world within the world. The yogis are not the only ones who taught that there are other dimensions to life. The apostle Paul chatted with a man, but was not sure whether the man was in the body or out it. This suggests that, even though he could see the man, there was sufficient evidence that he was not present in the usual sense.

As you awaken to the reality of what you are, you gain a passport that allows you entrance to what was off-limits before.

You cannot listen to FM or AM radio until you raise a proper antenna. Zen calls the body the receiving instrument. There are certain things you must know in order to tune your instrument for greater reception. The most important is worth repeating: Leave your knowledge at the door; God is not impressed with what you know. Know nothing, empty your mind, and stay in the posture of humility. The antenna contains nothing. It serves its purpose by being a still point in the emptiness.

XIX

Be an Antenna

Finally, you cannot break your soul from its prison of flesh—but it can be set free.

What you can do is provide the conditions that allow the miracle to take place.

The Twenty-third Psalm speaks to this clearly and beautifully: "The Lord is my shepherd . . . He leadeth me beside still waters. He restoreth my soul . . ."

Here, David bears witness to the fact that he enjoys nondoing. The Lord is leading, transforming his soul. David is simply receiving the blessing.

Lao Tzu teaches that the disciple of the Way should yield and overcome. Zen practitioners adopt the attitude and posture of Shakyamuni. They sit. This is no ordinary sitting. This is dynamic sitting, *zazen* or *shikantaza,* sitting in the attitude of faith.

If you believe that we move and have our being in God, are you willing to sit and wait until He comes into your consciousness and floods you with His presence? Are you willing to lay down your thoughts to experience the Real, to taste eternity and expand beyond the cosmos here and now? Are you willing to lay down your ego-mind and body, to be slain by the One who made you from the unimaginable? Are you willing to die to all that you know, with not a single familiar thing to hold onto? Do you have the faith to be obliterated? Do you believe enough to sit by the still waters and invite the tsunami to wash you away?

Only if you can answer yes to these questions are you ready for the journey through the gateless gate. Only then can the Christian go through Jesus to the Father. Only then can the Buddhist slay the Buddha to become Buddha. Only then can the Muslim reflect Allah through his eyes and His peace through his presence. Only then can the Jew remember that Jehovah is One God, the God of all men, that, ultimately, He of a thousand names has no name at all.

So if you would reach out across the void where I live, where Santji lives, you must remember that there is no living being on the earth, only matter.

This point was dramatically demonstrated in December 1997. I received the news from Janadevi of the California Temple of Cosmic Religion that Santji had entered Maha Samadhi. In layperson's terms, he had left this world. It was not expected. Only days before, I had talked to him where he was in India and, in retrospect, he spoke as if he were giving me my final blessings. He ended the talk with, "God bless your mission, Kitabu."

When Guruji met me in 1976, he called me Kitabu Krishnadas. Later, he would call me Kitabu Shyamadas. Both names connoted that I was a servant of God, as warrior/friend/lover of humanity. In the Himalayan tradition, a name points to the spirit of the person. A name change is given when warranted. In the final years, Sadguru Sant Keshavadas, whose name means "Realized Master, saint, who is servant of the Lord," gave me the designation Kitabu Kaivalya Shyam. The new name, simply translated, means Kitabu the Abode of the Lord. The name Kaivalya also translates as "absolute." It is not for me to elaborate on, but I do enjoy knowing that the name he gave me is of one who fights the forces of evil; I am no friend to demons.

I realize, however, that the church world has no sense of divine hierarchy, except in a limited sense. For Jesus Christ to be King of Kings, and Lord of Lords, there would have to be other kings and lords. Guruji also called him master of masters. Everyone has a job to do. Jesus did his, but each person, chosen or called to service, must give their all. Whitney Houston sang a song called "One Moment in Time" (written by Albert

Hammond and John Bettis), which says, "There will come one moment in time when everything depends on you."

Jesus passed that test. Only the Supreme Identity gives out such assignments. Jesus demonstrated the key: "Not my will." I don't have to understand this mystery, but I am happy to be a pawn of the One who made me. To be chosen is to have no choice but to fall, to fail, to hurt, to suffer again and again so God can work in your body/mind that which others will not allow Him to.

Hearing the news that I had lost the living manifestation who communicated with me as the Father-Nature of God, I went outside on the deck and looked into the heavens. The sky was filled with stars. "You left me here all alone," I cried out.

That night, I lay in bed and finally fell asleep. Suddenly, I sat bolt upright. My wife, Joyce, a Christian missionary, asked, "What's wrong?"

"Nothing," I said. "Santji just embraced me."

Indeed, when I fell asleep, I entered the dimension of the soul. Someone grabbed me from behind. I recognized the familiar and loving spirit of Santji. He felt the same way he did when he was in the physical. I knew now that what he told me in the beginning was the gospel. He said that we would never be apart. We needed no phones, no visible means of communication. The next day, I called Guru Rama Mataji, his wife and disciple of 40 years, and shared the experience. We had both inherited Dharma missions. We were now family more than ever.

Bodies, all bodies, are but dust in the eyes.

Sit the body down. Let your mind enter suspension. Rest. Let all thoughts pass as if they are nothing but drifting leaves carried by the gentle breeze, the same breeze breathing through you. Concentrate only on exhaling with your mind's eye pinpointed three inches below your navel. Be noble. You are spiritual royalty. Keep your back straight, let there be no strain, and your body will eventually fade from your awareness, maybe not on the first few tries, but eventually. Soon there will be no separation between your breath and the Breath that is God. There will be just breathing, inhaling and exhaling—but not you breathing, just the breathing universe. Breathe and keep the faith. One day the shell will fall away and your soul will be the pristine sun in a universe called you.

"To them that loved him, he gave the power to become the sons of God." God is spirit. His offspring are spirit. The choice is yours: You can continue to worship the mind and live only within the finite universe where death is certain; or you can surrender your limited understanding to the Unlimited, and soar beyond to worlds without end.

It is time now for the preachers to make room, for the priests, imams, and rabbis to step back a little. The Tathagathas are manifesting in the West. There is a job to be done. The teachers are here to close the book and raise the sword against the enemies of truth. We never turn back. You never see us coming. You never see us leave. We travel soul to soul in an endless universe where there is neither time nor space. The story of life never ends. There is just a new episode, a different adventure, on a channel you may not get.

God is the same yesterday, today, and tomorrow. The faces may change, but the spirit of truth never does. All the positions that ever were are still being played out on planet Earth. In the beginning, Man (Mind) became a living soul. Until you rediscover your primal root, what you call life will be a sad and poor pretender to the real thing. As long as you function from the assumed high point of intellect, you will never recognize the forces that manipulate your life by sabotaging your weakened spirit through the medium of your mind.

If you want to *be* the soul instead of just having one, you must seize your mind and slay all nine heads of the dragon at once.

This is not so hard. A dragon is an image. Be not conformed to the images of this world.

> Sit and breathe. Sit and breathe. The sun shines, the wind blows, rain falls from the sky. Sit and breathe. You heart beats, your blood flows. Sit and breathe. "Sitting still doing nothing, Spring comes and the grass grows by itself."
>
> —Vernon Kitabu Turner
> (also, a famous Zen phrase)

Enlightenment does not come by what we do. What we did blew the lights out in the first place. Sit still. There is a sweet healing coming down the line, Mind to mind. I bear witness to that light. Stay your mind on no thing. It is only a matter of time before the lights come on again "in the house of love."

One final point: What you desire for yourself you must desire for everyone because everyone is none other than you. We truly are one at the root. What goes around does come around. If you leave someone out of the healing of the mind and soul, that someone will inevitably be you.

From the first not a thing is.

I have a question, but don't try to answer it.

If there was nothing in the beginning,
what makes you so sure there is anything now?

When you are soul again, we will laugh about that.
Until that day comes. Sit still! Breathe!

Ahhhh!

About the Author

Vernon Kitabu Turner is a martial arts instructor and philosopher. He lives in Virginia Beach, Virginia.

Hampton Roads Publishing Company

. . . for the evolving human spirit

HAMPTON ROADS PUBLISHING COMPANY publishes books on a variety of subjects, including metaphysics, spirituality, health, visionary fiction, and other related topics.

For a copy of our latest trade catalog, call toll-free, 800-766-8009, or send your name and address to:

HAMPTON ROADS PUBLISHING COMPANY, INC.
1125 STONEY RIDGE ROAD • CHARLOTTESVILLE, VA 22902
e-mail: hrpc@hrpub.com • www.hrpub.com